Teach Your Children Well

To Jasmina
For the children

Teach Your Children Well

A Solution to Some of North America's Educational Problems

Michael Maloney

Michael Maloney

Cambridge Center for Behavioral Studies
Cambridge, MA

Cambridge Center for Behavioral Studies
1770 Massachusetts Avenue, #123
Cambridge, MA 02140
USA

Library of Congress Cataloging-in-Publication Data

Maloney, Michael, 1941-
    Teach your children well : a solution to some of North America's educational problems / Michael Maloney. -- 1st ed.
        p. cm.
    Contents: Includes bibliographical references and index.
    ISBN 1-881317-06-4 (pbk.)
    1. School improvement programs--Canada.   2. School improve-ment programs--United States.   3. Educational innovations--Canada.
4. Educational innovations--United States.   5. Alternative schools--Canada.   6. Alternative schools--United States.   7. Effective teach-ing.   I. Title.

LB2822.84.C2M35   1998
371.04--DC21   98-37879
                                                                                CIP

Printed by University of Toronto Press Incorporated

This book is dedicated to the memory of

Eric Christian Haughton
(1934 - 1985)

Friend, mentor, educator, researcher and
brother-in-arms in the war against illiteracy
and academic child abuse.

"The poor man is not he who is without a cent,
but he who is without a dream."

~ Harry Kemp

Contents

Note: For the purpose of clarity, the pronouns/adjective "he", "him" and "his" are used in the generic sense throughout this book. They are intended to be inclusive of both sexes.

Acknowledgments

As a rookie writer, I thought of this book as a work of art created solely by the author. I have come to learn, however, of the many influences and individuals that temper and enrich the writing and the final offering. They need to be acknowledged because *Teach Your Children Well* could not have happened without them. They are:

My principal mentors who gave me something to say: Ogden Lindsley, Zig Engelmann, Eric and Elizabeth Haughton, Linda Olen and Linda Youngmayr;

My watchful editors who helped me to say it more clearly: Lynne Brearley, ably assisted by Judie Preece, Laurie Coo, Rae Christie and Emmet Bresnahan;

My loyal center managers who did the work so that I could report it: Anne Desjardins, Pam Broad, Susan Burnie, David McKay, Tami DiCola, Susan Pearce, Donna Clarke, Teresa Boyle, Sherry Michelin, Tina Weiringa, Angela Jones, Anne Helferty, Gurpreet Grewal, Krista Darling, Chantal Zehr, Nancy Hoople, Helen Marentic, JoAnn Rose and Tadger Murray;

My entrepreneurial colleagues who expanded our work across North America and then sent us their contributions: Kent Johnson, Ian Spence and Aileen Stan-Spence, Elizabeth Haughton and Anne Desjardins;

My computer software partners who are launching our work into cyberspace as CyberSlate.ca: Michael Summers, Ian Spence and the National Research Council of Canada;

My daring publisher and my seasoned distributors: The Cambridge Center for Behavioral Studies, especially Betsy Constantine, its executive director; and Hushion House, especially Bill Hushion, its founder; and A.P.G.

A special thanks to those who shared their stories: "Madame" Lynne Brearley, Steve, Kim, Allison and Steffi Graf, Terry Harris, Clyde Snow, Crystal Del Zompo and Jamie Lyons.

Deep appreciation to Andrew Nikiforuk for his Foreword.

Foreword

Education can happen at school, and when it does, it can be a fairly dangerous and exciting event. But good learning - the essential foundation for any education - requires good teaching. And that's what this book is about: instruction that works, pure and simple.

Good teaching isn't a nuclear science but it is a lot more important. Its primary characteristics haven't changed much since the invention of the school.

For starters, good teaching assumes all children can be taught. It does so by breaking down ideas or skills into manageable bits. Good teaching is clear, direct and sequenced. As such, it has beginnings and ends. It not only shows children the logic of the subject at hand but then demands that students apply and practise it. Good teaching is also economical. There is no reason why children should spend three years learning how to read with wretched teaching if good teaching (and a good program) can get the job done in a year.

Unfortunately there is no shortage of bad teaching these days. Parents can find lots of it in most elementary schools, while students freely experience sloppy and ineffective instruction in university classrooms on a daily basis. Poor children or students with disabilities receive so much bad teaching that they often become experts on the subject. For some unknown reason North American educators tend to concentrate their most offensive teaching in academic skills. Most elementary students, for instance, stand a better chance of receiving more effective instruction on how to swim or play baseball than on how to read or spell.

This teaching deficit has the gravest impact on the poorest and most troubled children. A child coming from a home rich in intellectual capital can survive some of this nonsense. But a child who exits a home where nothing works, only to attend a public school where nothing matters, has been robbed twice. Many of these children, of course, spend the rest of their lives teaching society the high costs of bad schooling.

As Michael Maloney notes, none of this is acceptable or excusable. We know better and have known better for a long time. We can teach most children how to read or write without expanding the length of the school year or the amount of time or money we spend on schooling for that matter.

We can do this by training our teachers effectively and by making our schools more accountable for results. Good teachers, after all, are like good ecologists; they can predict the consequences of good actions in the classroom. Maloney wants to see more predictably good teaching, and I hope this prescriptive book furthers that important work.

Andrew Nikiforuk, Calgary, 1998

Preface

One in four North Americans can't read a newspaper. Eight percent of university graduates, eleven percent of college graduates and seventeen percent of high school graduates are illiterate, according to Canada's Council of Education Ministers. The situation is at least as bad in the United States.

For the last 25 years, Michael Maloney of QLC Educational Services and his colleagues in learning centers and schools across North America have been teaching such people to read, write, spell and do arithmetic in a matter of weeks or at most months. Illiterate adults are commonly made college-ready in a year or less and, once there, they survive better than public school graduates.

The methods employed by Maloney and his colleagues are in the public domain, are sold by major educational publishers, and are completely available to every school in both nations. These programs are supported by seventy-five years of combined empirical research including the largest, most expensive, long-term comparative study of educational methods in the Western world.

They are not only virtually ignored by public education, but in documented instances, schools and programs using these methods have been closed down, the teachers transferred and in some cases released from employment.

Illiteracy's abiding international disgrace occurs at the very time when politicians and school administrators beg for understanding and promise massive educational reform to get North Americans out of the lowest places on international tests.

Teach Your Children Well chronicles the history and current status of the successful efforts of Michael Maloney and his staff, the technologies, his associates and their stories. It analyzes the reasons for schools' rebuffing proven methods while simultaneously creating growing amounts of ignorance in millions of students at every level in the best-funded schools on the planet. It suggests options and ways they can be implemented so that the public school systems of North America can begin to *Teach Your Children Well*.

Part One

. . . .

The Beginnings

A Different Drummer ~ A Different Approach

* *

"Pioneers get the arrows; settlers get the land."
- Michael Maloney

Usually a person can point to the defining moment that changed all or part of his personal or professional life. Understanding those events gives us a clearer indication of who and what we are. For me, one instance stands out vividly as the point at which my career and my future life changed, although this became clear only in hindsight.

My Personal "Road to Damascus"

History reports that the Roman officer Saul, who came to be better known as St. Paul, had his blinding insight while traveling the road to Damascus. My defining moment was also a blinding insight.

In 1971, while lecturing at Loyalist College, one of Ontario's Community Colleges of Applied Arts and Sciences, I was asked by the recently formed Hastings County Board of Education to act as a psychological consultant.

A number of the board's teachers were reporting discipline problems with students in their classrooms. In response, the school district had asked two psychology professors from Queen's University to put together and supervise a group of local consultants who would assist these schools. Fortunately, the administration selected Dr. Ray Peters and Dr. Bill Marshall, both behaviorists. Ray and I had been in the same graduate program at the University of Waterloo in the late sixties and had worked on research projects for the same professors. Ray knew my background and orientation and recommended me to the team.

I was assigned to the rural schools in the northern part of what was then one of Ontario's largest school districts in terms of geographical area. I worked under the supervision of Frank Tate, the superintendent responsible for a dozen or so generally underserviced schools spread across those many hundreds of square kilometers. Frank was an old war horse, near the end of his career. He had a firm belief in his own decisions and he didn't much care who knew it. He was well-experienced, well-liked and generally right. Frank was guided by a simple precept, "If it's good for the kids, I'm all for it." He liked the idea of getting help for these teachers and kids and supported me from the outset.

The Challenge

My first challenge was Darwin, a Grade 7 student who was creating a constant uproar both inside and outside his classroom. He was inattentive and unproductive. Worse, he distracted the class, interfered with the lessons and was a general troublemaker on the playground. His teacher was at his wits' end and had requested help. Darwin had been disciplined, given detentions, kept in at recess, sent to the principal's office and sent home, all of the usual approaches, but none of which effected any lasting change.

On my first visit to his school, I sat in Darwin's classroom and noted that he could last about ten minutes without going off task. The search for a solution to this problem led me to a strategy known as the "Good Behavior Clock", first used by Dr. Edward Kubani of the University of Hawaii. The Good Behavior Clock is a kitchen timer set at intervals within a pre-determined period. This period of time is established by observing how long the student can work without incident. If the student is "working" when the timer rings, the entire class earns points toward some reward they and the student have chosen. This could be extra gym time, a night off from homework, etc.

As the behavior improves, the time periods become increasingly longer, until they match the school day and are faded out.

A plan based on Kubani's original study was drawn up, adapted to the teacher's satisfaction and implemented. A well-behaved student was selected each day to run the clock and record the points in order to free up the teacher so he could get on with teaching. When the timer went off, the teacher immediately looked at Darwin and made a decision as to whether or not he was "on task". If he was, the class was awarded a point and the teacher went back to the lesson.

The effect was dramatic and instantaneous. Since Darwin was the only one who could win points for the class, he became the center of attention for an entirely different reason, and for an entirely different set of behaviors. He became a star, loving this new role and all of the attention it brought. The kids encouraged his good behavior instead of provoking him into getting into trouble. Darwin stopped most of his distracting antics almost immediately, wasn't given detentions nor sent to the principal's office. He was becoming a model student. Everyone was pleased, including Frank Tate.

"The Lightning Bolt"

On one of my periodic visits to his classroom, I watched as Darwin and the other students worked on a math assignment. Darwin was being appropriate and after about ten minutes, I wandered down by his desk. His books were open, his pencil was in his hand and his paper was completely blank. Given that the work had been assigned at least ten minutes before, I asked him what he was having difficulty with and if I could help him. He looked up at me and said, "It's some of the words." I then asked him, "Which ones? I'll help you with them", to which he replied, "All of them." Darwin could not read.

I felt like I had been hit by a bolt of lightning. Here he was, sitting there being good, period after period, day after day - and learning nothing. I had solved his teacher's problem, his principal's problem, but I had completely failed Darwin.

The next day I began a search for effective reading programs at the Humphrey Library at Queen's University. I found reference to a project called "Follow Through" and the name of Siegfried Engelmann at the University of Oregon. It seemed he was one man who had been highly successful with children at risk of school failure.

My future had been determined the moment Darwin looked up at me and said, "All of them."

The Conversion

Darwin's plight had shaken me such that the following summer I flew to Oregon, walked into the Engelmann-Becker Corporation in Eugene and asked for Zig Engelmann. His participation in Project Follow Through as part of the University of Oregon's Direct Instruction model was clearly the best method currently available with any significant empirical data to support it. I asked him to teach me to teach children to read. His answer was classic Zig, "Third door on the right - the teacher's name is Linda."

For the next couple of weeks, with Linda Olen as my mentor, I learned the fundamentals of the approach developed by Engelmann, Wes Becker and the rest of the Oregon research team.

In September, I asked Frank Tate to help me start some pilot programs in his schools, one of which was to include Darwin. Frank agreed, and the beginning of what was to become my new career was launched. In January of that year I left college teaching to return to the trenches of the public schools, armed with a new set of tools to help teachers and kids.

The Other Shoe Drops

When I joined the Hastings County Board as a full-time member of Frank Tate's support team in January of 1972, I had the good fortune to meet Eric Haughton, an educational psychologist who had just given up a career at York University (Toronto) to work directly with teachers and children. Eric and his wife, Elizabeth, were destined to become another major influence in my professional life. Eric had completed his doctoral degree several years before at the University of Kansas with Dr. Ogden R. Lindsley, the creator of Precision Teaching. This methodology, although not part of the Follow Through project, had a long, strong body of empirical research to support it.

Precision Teaching is primarily a measurement system which allows the teacher and/or learner to pinpoint academic or other performances and measure them accurately in a couple of minutes. The teacher simply specifies the behavior of interest, such as reading, and determines its rate and accuracy. The learner's performance is compared to a known standard. A level of good, competent reading would be 200 words per minute with no more than 2 errors. The student's score is recorded on the Standard Celeration Chart (a.k.a. Standard Behavior Chart), the workhorse of Precision Teaching. If the performance increases, the program continues. If the performance stalls or decreases, the data on the chart indicate the need for intervention, and changes can be implemented immediately.

It is an elegant system which can be taught to children as young as those in Grade 1. It lets them be actively involved in tracking their own learning. It also allows them to be an integral part of the decision-making when changes are needed. Its attributes, history, research and effectiveness are covered in detail in Chapter 9.

Eric showed me the fundamentals of Precision Teaching and I outlined to him the concepts and applications of Direct Instruction. Each of us realized that by combining these technologies, we could most likely create faster and more efficient learning.

Combining Forces

The Haughtons worked on a different teacher support team in schools located mostly within the city of Belleville. Their superintendent, Wally Beevor, was, in some ways, the direct opposite of Frank Tate. He was young, eager, ambitious, and just beginning his career as a superintendent. He was determined to make a difference. Like Frank, he cared most about the kids and less about the administration and whose feathers he might ruffle. He and Frank saw the advantages of these two technologies and joined forces to promote them into Hastings County classrooms from an administrative level. Their support allowed Eric and me to accomplish a number of things. We were able to arrange conferences for teacher training for both technologies. The Direct Instruction sessions, on two occasions, featured Zig Engelmann himself as the trainer. Zig spent an entire week visiting Direct Instruction programs in classrooms and working directly with the teachers involved.

We hired Linda Olen, my original trainer, and another of the Follow Through trainers, Linda Youngmayr, to come from Oregon and work with our support teams to help implement Direct Instruction programs in various classrooms.

Getting Student Performance Data

We began to set up a data-gathering system in our schools. Teachers provided data on each child in their classrooms from three one-minute samples of academic performance. The topics involved oral reading, math facts and writing. This set of data was collected once each month and provided to each principal who in turn reported it to Frank or Wally at their regular principals' meetings. The collection of data was then collated for the entire group of schools so that progress could be tracked over each month of the school year.

The process took very limited teacher time and effort: a one-minute sample of reading for each child, a one-minute sample of writing the answers to math facts and a one-minute writing sample. Only a few minutes were required to record the student's scores for the month.

The data, however, provided interesting and powerful information. Children's performances could be compared to a goal for each activity. Their results could be directly compared on a monthly basis by grade level, by school, by specific classroom, or even by the individual child over time on one or more of the same tasks. These data could reveal which students in which classrooms were performing above the expected levels, at the expected levels and most importantly, which pupils were not improving and therefore needed help. For some teachers, such data constituted a threat, and was actively resisted.

End of an Era

Unfortunately, Frank Tate retired and Wally Beevor became the Director of another school board. Eric and I lost our administrative influence, and the following year our contracts were not renewed. Linda Olen and Linda Youngmayr were also removed from the support teams. Elizabeth Haughton returned to a classroom and the project collapsed from lack of support. Some teachers continued to use the tools we had provided, but as they left the system, the technology fell into disuse and can no longer be found in Hastings County.

What Happened to the Others?

I was devastated by the Board's decision to cut back on its support staff. I thought we had proven our usefulness beyond question and would get a chance to continue implementing methods that showed such clear-cut gains for kids. I was wrong. And the price to be paid was my career in public education.

I had always been politically active, both outside of organized political parties (with such issues as the Vietnam War) and within such parties. I completely understood the consequences of not having power on one's side. I began to wonder what we might have done to prevent or avoid the discontinuation of behavioral technologies in our school district. The results spoke for themselves. The politics had obviously needed much more attention than we had given it.

I began to search for other places in Canada and the United States where Direct Instruction or Precision Teaching had been used by a public school district at a system level. I wanted to know if anything had been done differently in order to survive and be successful. I did not find any such instances. I did, however, find a number of attempts like the one we had made in Hastings County. All of them had failed, usually within a few years.

Other System-Wide Implementations

At one point in the early seventies, School District #10 in Chicago had attempted to introduce Direct Instruction across its schools. The venture failed within three years. The same thing happened with a district-wide D.I. project initiated by Maria Martinaro in Houston, Texas. A smaller implementation failed after a couple of years in London, Ontario.

The Sacajawea Project was the largest implementation of Precision Teaching and included all of the schools of Montana. It was discontinued after twelve years of consistent, heady, academic success.

Also in the early seventies, Shlomo Cohen had attempted a combined Behavior Analysis/Direct Instruction project as a special education thrust in the ten schools of Portland, Maine. Within three years, the project ended and Shlomo Cohen, the Director of Special Education, and his Assistant Director, Carmen Marcy, were both gone.

While it is heartbreaking to see such successful projects discontinued, some are more disappointing than others. Perhaps the most tragic example of the failure of systems to adopt and use these proven technologies can be seen in the Speed Alternative School in South Chicago. The program was designed and implemented in the eighties by Carmen Marcy, one of Engelmann's doctoral graduates and the former Assistant Director of Special Education in Portland, Maine.

Working with the "Toughest to Teach" Students

When the Portland School venture collapsed, Carmen Marcy moved to Chicago to take on a new challenge. She was offered the principalship of a school in South Chicago, in one of its tougher areas. Speed Alternative School serviced fourteen schools in southern Cook and northern Wills counties. The assignment was to administer an alternative high school program for adolescents who could not cope with a regular secondary school setting or curriculum. Speed Alternative School had one special feature. Its student body would be comprised completely of students with juvenile records, the most serious behavior problem kids from these two districts. They were to be concentrated in a single school in an attempt to provide them with an opportunity to reconstruct their academic lives. All of these students had been through the court system many times. All of them were school failures.

I had the opportunity to visit Speed Alternative School to present workshops for Carmen's staff in Precision Teaching. Although the students were demonstrating many changes, there were still problems to be resolved. The morning before I arrived, two students had held up a corner store on their way to school. The previous week, one student had pulled a gun on another student and threatened to kill him. These were not cooperative, easy to teach, respectful kids. These were hard cases.

More Behavioral Practices

Parts of the program Carmen implemented were based on the applied behavioral practices used in the Anne Arundel Learning Center model developed by Shlomo Cohen and used successfully with pre-delinquent adolescents. The Speed Alternative School's program provided educational services to approximately sixty students using six teachers and six classroom aides. The school concentrated on teaching the fundamental academic skills required for the smooth transition into regular secondary school courses. Direct Instruction programs and practices were used whenever possible.

The academic success of these students was remarkable. Reports of progress to the administration based on standardized testing showed average gains in reading to be almost four months of progress for each month of instruction. Similar results occurred in other areas of curriculum.

A second major objective was to get the unacceptable social behavior of these students under control both inside the school and out in their community. This social skills program included parent training and home visits by school staff, so that the same practices used at school could be available to the parent(s) at home. The consistent application of the program's techniques resulted in students learning appropriate social and interpersonal behaviors, allowing them to function acceptably in a classroom and in their homes.

As a result of the diligent work done by Carmen Marcy and her capable, dedicated staff, Speed Alternative School was able to reduce the recidivism rate of these students to the courts by approximately 75% over a three-year period. More importantly, S.A.S. taught these seriously delinquent students the level of academic and social skills which provided them an opportunity to change their lives.

Unfortunately, like many other exemplary programs in which these technologies have been rigorously and successfully applied, the school was discontinued, and another golden opportunity to change students' lives was squandered. The boards considered the cost of the program too high. But how much have we paid in court costs, prison costs and broken lives as a result?

Last Man Standing

There is one setting where Direct Instruction has been implemented and has survived for twenty years. The remarkable progress of students from the Mabel B. Wesley School in Houston was discovered and reported by William Raspberry*, a Pulitzer Prize winning columnist for the *Washington Post* (March 1998) and in the June 1 issue of *National Review* in an article by Richard Nadler, the editor of *K.C. Jones Monthly*, a mid-western opinion journal.

The school is located in Houston's inner city and has a student population that is 92% African-American and 7% Hispanic. This is an impoverished student body. Eighty-two percent of the students qualify for subsidized lunches. Despite their low socio-economic conditions, the first graders rank in

* Raspberry's article resulted from his reading the book, *What Works in Education*, available from the Cambridge Center for Behavioral Studies.

the 82nd percentile in reading against all other schools in the district. A large number of its students, thirty-one out of thirty-two in one class alone, have gone to Houston's gifted and talented program. And according to the article, Doug Carnine reported that their knowledge of how the basic body systems work was on a par with that of entering freshmen at Baylor Medical School. The same results have been produced over many years. Its principal, Thaddeus Lott, has been a Direct Instruction devotee for over two decades. His students' achievements were so superlative that he was even accused of cheating on the tests! Unfortunately, he is no longer at Mabel B. Wesley but has become the principal of a group of charter schools in Houston.

It will be interesting to see the future performance of Wesley Public School without Thaddeus Lott at the helm, and to see whether or not the D.I. programs survive. It will be equally interesting to see the achievements of the charter schools which Thaddeus Lott now looks after. The before-and-after pictures of the progress of the students in both settings will tell a great deal about the effectiveness of the Direct Instruction method. I'll put my money squarely on Thaddeus Lott. I'd even offer odds.

Next Steps

When I was cut loose from Hastings County, I was asked to apply for an interview to be an elementary school principal in Portland, Maine.

A major sea change was underway in the schools of this New England city. A new superintendent*, Ron Raynolds, had just been hired with a mandate to improve the academic performance of students in its ten schools. At the time, annual test scores for Portland students were at or near the bottom of results for the state of Maine, the state itself ranking well down on those for the nation. Raynold's directive to the principals was to make any necessary changes, ask for any support,

---

* A superintendent in American schools is the top management official hired by the board. His subordinates are directors. The terms are reversed in Canadian school boards.

implement any programs, but to get the job done within a couple of years or pay with their jobs. After two years, when little or no change occurred in three of his ten schools, Raynolds sacked the principals and went headhunting for their replacements. Two of the schools were in the more well-to-do suburban areas of Portland. The third, North Public, was a dilapidated, inner-city school with a bad reputation and a high concentration of "at-risk" kids.

An Interesting Interview Procedure

I was invited to apply by Shlomo Cohen and was granted an interview. The interview process was without doubt a model which bears examination. I had never seen such a process before, nor have I heard of it since. But it did appeal to me and I could see it being used much more widely in public schools.

Each candidate met with seven groups of interviewers. One set was from the central administration, three sets were from the staffs of the three hiring schools and the remaining three sets consisted of parents from the three schools involved. Each group interviewed the applicants and scored their performance, asking questions and noting responses. At the end of the seven interviews, the scores for each of the applicants were compiled and the three highest scoring candidates were offered the jobs in the order in which they finished in the rankings. To everyone's surprise, when given first choice, I asked to become the new principal of North Public on the premise that with kids who were at the bottom of the list, I could create more positive academic change than with their middle-class peers, many of whom were already doing relatively well.

Unfortunately, despite becoming professionally certified in the State of Maine, and despite everyone's best efforts, I was unable to obtain the necessary landed-immigrant status and work permits, and was forced to give up North School and return to Canada. A year later, Ron Raynolds was appointed Commissioner of Education for Alaska and within three years, the Portland endeavor was over.

Going Private - Starting Quinte Learning Center

It was clear to me by 1978 that public schools in Canada and the USA were not about to embrace behavioral approaches to education, despite the overwhelming data regarding their effectiveness. If I wanted to continue to work with children at risk of school failure, I was going to have to do so outside of the public school domain.

I decided that if these technologies were really as good as I thought they were, they should be able to be sold in the marketplace. The problem of children and adults failing to learn to read, write and do arithmetic had not gone away. If anything, it was becoming more prevalent. If I could provide these services privately, and convince parents to pay for them, I could continue to teach the way I wanted. In September, 1978, I returned to Belleville, and in January, 1979, I opened my learning center.

Opening a private learning center in which you attempt to sell services for which the public has already paid in their taxes is not a formula to get rich. But when parents cannot get the service they need, they will, in fact, go elsewhere and buy it. The learning center grew slowly, scraping out an existence, meeting its payroll and its bills, but little more. Although no roaring financial success, the parents loved it. After two years of providing after-school tutorials, day-time literacy programs for adults and summer-school sessions for children, we were being pressured to start a full-time day school. With competent staff like Anne Desjardins and Pam Broad, I decided to take the risk and open a full-time day school for children who were unsuccessful in regular public school classrooms. We rented two classrooms of a centrally located school that had recently been closed by the local Board. Having the students all day, every day, allowed us the chance to try a full-blown implementation of the three technologies that we had originally started to use in Hastings County - Direct Instruction, Precision Teaching and Behavior Management. The results of this integration are outlined in considerable detail in Chapter 11.

Helping Others Get Started

As the Quinte Learning Center started to take root and produce results, we began to share our research findings in presentations at professional conferences. One of my key staff in this
role was Anne Desjardins. Anne was not only a superb teacher, she was also very adept at collecting and using data and was
very easy to listen to. Our work began to be presented at the
Association for Behavior Analysis international conferences,
sometimes with our colleague, Eric Haughton. Several people
showed an interest in visiting our center, and over the next
few years, we were able to assist some of these individuals in
starting similar learning centers in both Canada and the
USA. Their stories are told in Chapter 12.

The Software Period

In the early 1980s, the personal computer made its way
into North American classrooms. One of the biggest, most
powerful and most pervasive bandwagons ever to hit education had rolled into town. It is still a growing issue in schools
after more than fifteen years. It had much the same impact on
the Quinte Learning Center as it had on many other schools
and many other teachers.

Our concern was that, although they were expensive, we
needed to have classroom computers like any other school.
We could remediate the academic problems of the children
but feared sending them back to a public-school classroom
where they might be the only pupils who were not computer-
literate. If that happened, they would once again look and feel
different from the other students.

As a solution, we purchased three computers and began
the search for some useful software, only to find that very little, if any, existed. Innocently enough, we decided to design
and build our own programs. If we could drop our technologies
onto a disk, we could sell it and impact the skills of hundreds,
perhaps thousands of students.

Mighty Math

Our first effort, like that of many educational software developers in the early 1980s, was in arithmetic programs. This probably happened because math is lawful and not idiomatic like reading, spelling or grammar. We created *Mighty Math* based on the principles of Precision Teaching, and began marketing it in Utah, where Precision Teaching was popular. *Mighty Math* accurately practiced and evaluated the basic arithmetic operations of addition, subtraction, multiplication and division. It rewarded improved performance with a choice of math games, kept records for each student's attempts and even made data-based decisions and program changes appropriate to the student's level of skill.

We drew the attention of several publishers, including Scholastic Inc. of New York, the largest publisher of educational software at that time. Most people recognize Scholastic for its in-school book fairs each year. In the seventies, they ventured into the growing business of educational software. Scholastic agreed to market *Mighty Math* in Canada and negotiated a series of instructional computer programs in arithmetic which came to be known as *Math Tutor*.

Math Tutor

Math Tutor is a series of eight computer programs which are instructional in nature. It is Direct Instruction on a disk. It actually teaches children or adults how to do any or all of the basic arithmetic operations taught in elementary school, with the exception of measurement, geometry and word problems. It has one feature which earmarks it as a leading edge technology - it analyzes and corrects errors as the student works. A comic figure, appropriately known as Ziggy, appears on the screen if you make an error. He shows you how to do the problem and then walks you through the exercise step-by-step before giving you a chance to do it independently.

Math Tutor took all of our time, money and energy. Anne Desjardins moved to Seattle to help our first visitor, Kent Johnson, develop Morningside Learning Center, and we discontinued the full-time day school. Pam Broad took a job at Loyalist College, the institution I had left to start all of this. Until 1989, Michael Summers and I would build a computer software development company. *Math Tutor* sold well and received international acclaim, including the Parent's Choice Award. Literally thousands of children have learned better math skills as a result of *Math Tutor*. It has remained on the market without any upgrades or changes for more than a decade.

Once *Math Tutor* was completed, we were commissioned by Scholastic to create a similar series of programs for language arts, but could not concur on its design and so we ended our agreement with them. Having kept the offshore rights to *Math Tutor*, we had a short fling at attempting to market it in Europe. European elementary schools had few computers, and those which they did have were used expressly to teach applications like word processing, spreadsheets and database management, not curriculum content. After a few months, we returned to Belleville to expand our core business in developing new learning centers.

Teaching Adults

Beginning in 1991, the Workers' Compensation Board of Ontario began to refer injured workers in need of academic retraining to Quinte Learning Center. The day-time programs expanded dramatically. In many instances, new classrooms had to be added and new centers opened. Within two years the company had grown to ten centers across the province of Ontario with more than 100 staff.

These clients needed one or more of three different types of programs offered at the Quinte Learning Center: basic literacy skills, secondary-school upgrading programs to prepare for college-level courses or training, and in some cases, English as a Second Language to teach fundamental speaking and listening skills.

As usual, we employed the three behavioral technologies, except in the upgrading program. Better than 85% of our clients successfully completed their courses. Many of these clients were then registered in community college programs or in job placement services. Statistics gathered in 1992 and 1993 indicate that those QLC students attending college had a drop-out rate of 8% as opposed to almost 50% for students from regular public high-school programs. Some of this is undoubtedly due to the maturity and motivation these students brought with them, but much is also due to the effectiveness of the instruction which amply prepared them for the challenges of their new placements.

The Research

Throughout our development history as learning centers, a school, and software creators, we continued doing applied research and presenting the results at conferences in Canada, the United States and Europe. We attempted to bring together the various players and share our data.

Perhaps the best and most memorable of these was a presentation at the Association for Behavior Analysis conference in Milwaukee in 1982. Zig Engelmann, the creator of Direct Instruction, shared the stage with Ogden Lindsley, the creator of Precision Teaching. These two men had never presented together before, despite their significant impact on the research of applied education. Eric Haughton acted as moderator and Anne Desjardins as the teacher supplying the research results from the Quinte Learning Center.

The room bulged at the seams as these two educational revolutionaries discussed the data from the first integration of their methods in a classroom of children at risk. Our students had gained well over two years of learning in one. This was the first presentation of their accomplishments at a major international conference. The analysis and feedback from the creators kept the capacity crowd awed to the point where the following workshop was delayed because people simply would not allow them off the podium. Since that presentation, an informal network of users of these technologies has begun to develop and share resources. Similar conferences have been held and the best of both worlds has come to more teachers and classrooms.

The Three Technologies

Our experience has shown us that there exists a set of proven methods that can dramatically alter the problems of illiteracy and innumeracy. They are almost completely foreign to the daily experience of most classroom teachers across North America, to most teacher-training programs and institutions, and to most school administrators and school board trustees.

What are these methods? Just what is Direct Instruction? Precision Teaching? Applied Behavior Management? The description of these technologies is reported throughout various parts of this book. Part Four more specifically describes and analyzes these systems and their research. Part Six attempts to determine why they are not part of your child's school experience, why they should be and what you can do to help make that happen. The burning question is obvious - "If they're so good, why don't we use them in every school?"

Understanding the Problem

In order to appreciate the need for the use of effective technology in classrooms, we must first understand the present situation, the current problems and the changes that are now underway in school systems across Canada and the United States. The greatest single problem in North American schools lies in their failure to produce competent or even literate students consistently. We need to investigate these concerns as a starting point for examining how schools are operating and how they should ideally function.

Part Two

· ·

The Problem

Illiteracy and Innumeracy
~The Growing Problem

• •

"Nothing is more terrible than to see ignorance in action."
- Goethe

What is Literacy?

In any discussion of the current state of literacy, we have to define what we are talking about. One of the confounding factors in the entire literacy debate is the lack of any standard definition of what literacy is or how it is measured. Where do we start? The most logical place to begin is with the existing research studies to see if we can get a handle on the breadth and depth of the problem. There is an abundance of literature on the subject spanning many decades. For our purposes a sample of several of the major studies in Canada and the U.S. is described below.

The Study of Illiteracy in America - A Numbers Game

One of the more recent sources of information on literacy at a national level in the U.S. is the National Assessment of Educational Progress (NAEP), a project funded by the Office of Educational Research and Improvement. The grant was given to the Educational Testing Service of Princeton, New Jersey. The project was mandated by the U.S. Congress to collect data over a period of time on American students in several areas of learning and to make the data and reports available to federal, state and local education agencies.

The Major Findings

The panel of experts who designed the framework for the NAEP study formulated a definition of literacy as follows:

"Using printed and written information to function in society, to achieve one's goals and to develop one's knowledge and potential."

In defining literacy, the experts considered that it pertains to three distinct categories: prose, document and quantitative. Prose literacy constitutes being able to deal with information found in newspapers, magazines and periodicals, including poetry. Document literacy refers to the ability to read and understand such documents as job or credit applications, bus schedules, maps and telephone books. Quantitative literacy deals with computing numerical information, such as balancing a check book, calculating a fare, or filling out an order form.

Foremost among NAEP's major findings was that America was now more literate than at any time in its history.

Literacy's Changing Benchmark

While this major finding may sound encouraging, it is worthwhile to remember that the benchmark for measuring literacy has changed in an upward direction in the U.S. over the last century. A hundred years ago, people were considered literate if they could sign their name instead of making an "X".

During the First World War, screening of recruits led to the development of the entire field of tests and measurement which exists today. It was an attempt to differentiate recruits and draftees into groups with various skill levels and aptitudes. It also wished to provide personnel for training in more advanced tasks in all areas of the armed forces. Those who did not fare well on the tests tended to wind up as infantry in the forward trenches. More literate individuals found their way into such activities as gunnery school, navigation courses and other more technical, generally less lethal pursuits. Even at this time, literacy was not evenly distributed. It was clear that recruits and draftees from some states tended to do better than those from some other states which, at the time, had inferior education systems. This finding is reported by E.D. Hirsch (1996) in an analysis by Bagley who reviewed the Army Alpha test scores of 170,000 WW I soldiers and found a very high correlation (.74) between the soldiers' home states and the test scores. Soldiers from states like Massachusetts and Oregon, which had relatively better schools, scored significantly higher on the test than groups of men from Mississippi or Alabama. African-Americans from states with highly ranked schools had higher I.Q.s than white soldiers from low-ranking school states. Such results tend to strengthen the idea that high-quality schools can erase other cultural differences, such as race or socio-economic background.

In the period of the Second World War, 95% of young adults were estimated to meet or exceed the performance of Grade 4 students.

During the period between 1940 and 1970, no statistics were kept on literacy levels by the U.S. Census Bureau.

By the War on Poverty period in the seventies, 80% of American youth was seen to be performing at an eighth grade level.

The report concludes that America should celebrate its success, but tempers the salutary remarks with the caution that there is still much to be done to transform America's youth into functional and skillful participants in the coming Information Age.

Other Notable Findings

If this analysis sounds somewhat rosy, a darker side becomes apparent when the data are more carefully scrutinized. These data show that while most young Americans were successful at the lower levels of each of the three scales that comprised the test, the numbers of literate young adults deteriorated quickly as the upper levels of the scales were reached.

Also, those youths who dropped out of school and/or were members of minorities, did more poorly than others. Young

African-Americans tended to fall nearer the bottom of the scales, Hispanics clustered nearer the middle, with whites near the upper end of the levels reached.

The report indicated that young adults generally performed significantly better on the reading scales than current 17-year-olds. The authors suggest that real-life experience assists in developing literacy. These data also lend themselves to the interpretation that the slide in literacy is continuing and, as a result, the 17-year-olds were simply even less skilled than the young adults were at the same age.

The report concludes that while most American youth have some degree of literacy skills that are greater than ever before, relatively small proportions are seen to be proficient at the moderate or complex tasks included in the study. The question of the ability of these individuals to benefit from post-secondary education or advanced training is also raised. The warning bell is sounded that unless something is done now to reverse the current situation, the pool of competent youth to manage the nation will continue to shrink in the next millennium, especially vis-à-vis the management of its technical affairs.

While the study questions the effectiveness of current educational practices to teach literacy, it does not recommend specific measures or methods.

The Critics

Finding Fault in the U.S.

As expected, the research on illiteracy does have its fair share of critics on both sides of the Canada - U.S. border. Jonathan Kozol may be the most recognized and widely-read American critic. His book, *Illiterate America*, has become a well-deserved centerpiece in the illiteracy debate because of its extensive analysis of the problem. Kozol has personal experience with illiterate youth and his criticism of the current state of public education is straightforward.

Kozol criticizes the NAEP report and others like it for presenting a statistical soup of results that would confuse even the most literate adults. He notes that the estimated numbers of illiterates fluctuates wildly from study to study, ranging from 10 million in the NAEP I study to 21 million in the U.S. Census bureau data to 70 million who cannot read at a grade 11 level (NAEP II study).

He is also enraged that these results should call for any kind of celebration. He argues that American youth is literate only when measured against yesterday's standards or Third World countries.

Kozol estimates that there are at least 25-30 million people in the USA who are currently reading below a fifth-grade level and another 35 million who are reading below a ninth-grade level - a total of sixty million illiterate or semi-literate Americans. He says that of this estimated sixty million, 50% (thirty million) are Hispanics, 44% (approximately twenty-six million) are blacks and 16% (10 million) are whites. He also points out that the numbers are rising with each report, projecting illiteracy among blacks to be beyond 50% in the 1990s. The U.S. ranked 49th of 158 member nations of the UN in literacy.

Kozol goes on to point out several rather disturbing findings that did not make it to the front page news reports about the Princeton study. Among those findings were indications that 40% of American adults cannot read a road map and 80% cannot calculate a tip in a restaurant or use a public transport route schedule.

He outlines the impact of illiteracy as a case study in its direct effects on one very small area, the publishing industry. Book sales per capita in the U.S. have dropped to 24th worldwide and numerous publishing houses have gone out of business. Only 30 cities in the U.S. have two or more daily newspapers, down from 181 cities in 1947. More than 50 major daily papers folded in the last 20 years.

A Canadian Study - A Mirror Image

The problem of illiteracy knows nothing of geographical

borders, so it is not surprising that illiterate individuals are also seen as a major educational issue in Canada. The most recent national study of illiteracy for which a report is available is the 1988 Council of Ministers of Education study of adult illiteracy in Canada (Cairns, 1988).The Council of Ministers is comprised of the Ministers of Education of the ten provinces and the emerging territories.

Again the study sets out a definition for illiteracy. The illiterate person is someone who can barely read or write (basic illiterates). Those whose reading, writing and number skills are not sufficient to get by in everyday life are considered functional illiterates.

The research shows that the real incidence of illiteracy is "higher than previously estimated". The study cites figures indicating that 24% of all adult Canadians (eighteen years or older) are completely or functionally illiterate, a total of four and a half million adults. The author also notes that a further 9%, or another 1.7 million, are only marginally literate, yielding almost 6 million illiterate adults in a country of 25,000,000 people, at least a quarter of whom are less than 18 years of age.

Given that this study was sponsored by the very people who are ultimately responsible for the educational well-being of the Canadian citizenry, it is highly unlikely that these results would be exaggerated or overstated.

Again, like the NAEP study, this research calls into question the effectiveness of the schools, pointing out a correlation between the rate of illiteracy and the high school drop-out rate, both at 24%. And like the NAEP study, the author finds some comfort in the fact that almost two million Canadians achieve functional literacy and are coping with society's requirements, even without completing a Grade 9 level in high school.

A Few Startling Facts

As with the NAEP study, on closer inspection, there are a few startling statistics in the data, namely, that 53% of students in Grades 5-8 are functionally illiterate, that 17% of high school graduates, 11% of community college graduates and 8% of university graduates are illiterate as measured by the definition of this study.

Reprinted by permission of The Globe and Mail

Canadian Critics

The existing state of Canadian education has spawned its share of critics, most notably, Dr. Joe Freedman, Dr. Harold Stevenson and Andrew Nikiforuk, the former educational columnist for Canada's first national newspaper, *The Globe and Mail*.

Dr. Joe Freedman, a Calgary physician, founded the Society for Advancing Educational Research and has spoken and written widely on the failures of Canadian elementary and secondary school education.

Andrew Nikiforuk outlines his concerns in his 1993 book, *School's Out*. Although told from a Canadian perspective, using Canadian statistics, there are striking similarities in the criticisms and proposed solutions of the educational watchdogs on both sides of the 49th parallel.

Nikiforuk reports on the results of another major Canadian literacy study done by the Southam Press in 1987. It determined that 24% of Canadian youth cannot read well and that 17% of high school graduates are illiterate. He further reports a Statistics Canada study of 1989 indicating that 33% of Canadian high school graduates could not meet everyday reading demands.

The Canadian Teachers' Federation reported that more than 43% of its teachers surveyed felt that the "quality of literacy" among students was lower today than it had been a decade earlier.

The Economic Council of Canada in its 1992 report, *A Lot to Learn: Education and Training in Canada*, predicts that there will be 2,000,000 illiterate students in this country by the year 2000.

North America and the International Scene

The comparison of the performances of North American students against those of other nations adds more fuel to the fire that is turning our schools to toast. Freedman points out the poor performance of children and young adults in basic skills as reflected in the results of international tests in which most of the Canadian provinces participated. Canadian students placed at or near the bottom of the distributions of scores.

In 1982 and 1988, both Canada and the U.S. were part of the International Mathematics Studies in which, although Canada finished ahead of the U.S., both were in the bottom half of the scores for all countries participating.

Our two nations were also part of both the 1988 and 1991 International Assessment of Educational Progress (IAEP) and, again, reported dismal results. Canada ranked ninth of fourteen countries in the study, with the U.S. in last place just after Spain and Slovenia.

Critics of international surveys complain that countries like Korea, Taiwan and Japan fare well in these comparisons because they select only the highest stream of academic students to write such tests. But most Canadian and U.S. schools involve streaming as well, although it is less stringent than in most Pacific Rim countries.

These criticisms lose much of their sting in the face of a study by Dr. Harold Stevenson (1992) in which the effect of selective student participation was controlled. Even with this variable controlled, the results of Grade 11 math skills still clearly indicate that North American students are at or near the bottom of the distribution of scores and cannot compete successfully in the global educational arena.

Furthermore, the international tests were constructed using curriculum which all participating countries had covered. It is the lowest common denominator of curriculum content. In countries such as Germany, Switzerland and the Pacific Rim nations, students in the same grade had already covered more advanced topics which went untested. Had these been included, the differences would most likely have been even more pronounced.

Within Country Comparisons

There is also a good deal of data in both Canada and the U.S. showing the relative positions of school districts, and of states and provinces on a variety of scholastic achievement tests in several subjects. Culling through that data would only allow us to pick the best of a bad bunch and is beyond the scope of this book.

If there is one observation to be drawn from such statistics, it would be the relatively low correlation between the amount of money spent per student and the academic results it generates. Ontario, Canada's richest and most populous province, spends more money on education than almost any other Canadian province and is ranked seventh out of the ten provinces in the 1991 IAEP study.

Conclusion

There may be several explanations for the data found in these and numerous other studies of illiteracy. The fact remains that at the end of the day, no matter how these studies define illiteracy, or sample and collect data, or analyze and present results, there has been, and continues to be, a significant problem with even the most fundamental education product created in North America.

The cost of such failure is as expensive as it is pervasive. These costs are the topic of the next chapter.

The Spiraling Cost of Ignorance

● ●

"If you think education is expensive, try ignorance."
- Bumper Sticker

What are the financial and human costs of the education system's failure to provide a quarter to a third of our citizens with less than adequate skills in reading, writing, spelling and arithmetic? This chapter attempts to outline some of the major costs and the societal impact of illiteracy. According to McGrady (1994), the American Library Association has estimated the cost of illiteracy at $224 billion annually. The Conference Board, an American business association, estimated that business losses alone top $25 billion per year.

Dr. Carl Kline, a child psychiatrist and Professor Emeritus of the University of British Columbia, originally practiced in Milwaukee, then in Vancouver. He points out that 69% of all prisoners, 85% of all unwed mothers, 79% of all welfare recipients, and 85% of all school dropouts are illiterate. Because these people remain as the tattered edges of our social fabric, our social services are stretched to the limit. Kline blames the lack of sufficient teacher training, not the teachers themselves, for these failures.

Given hard evidence of the problem, we must first establish that our poor performance cannot be left at the door of the taxpayers who fund education. Both the United States and Canada spend more money on education as a part of their GNP than most other countries in the world. As a benchmark, the province of Ontario spends close to $17 billion dollars from kindergarten to the end of secondary school. For the past several decades, most of this has gone into an average expenditure of almost $7000 annually for each of Ontario's 2.1 million public school students. Current government cutbacks will significantly reduce these levels of funding and will result in the reduction or cessation of necessary instructional programs. It will also provide the school administration with a handy tool to explain their continuing dismal results.

Costs of schooling in most U.S. states are slightly lower than this, but still roughly comparable. Both countries are above the mean for educational spending when compared to their European and Asian counterparts. The failure to provide adequate skills stems from other reasons and has created socially debilitating effects as outlined by a number of authors.

Illiteracy and Crime

Jonathan Kozol contends that there is a direct link between illiteracy and the crimes of 260,000 of the almost one-half million inmates in American state and federal prisons. The incarceration costs generate an expenditure of almost seven billion dollars annually.

In Canada, it now costs more than $50,000 every year to house each of its federal and provincial inmates, 85% of whom are illiterate or semi-literate.

Among these figures are the court and the legal costs required to prosecute these thousands of perpetrators, most of whom are supported by legal aid programs. Court and legal fees are estimated to be greater than the actual costs of incarceration. As for the victims, the monetary cost alone, though unestimated, would certainly be many additional millions of dollars.

Additional Schooling Costs

As well as the funds to support regular public school classrooms, school boards and related educational services across North America spend several billion dollars annually in special educational services for "at-risk" children who have been unaffected by regular classroom teaching of the basics. A significant portion of these expenditures is not a result of any particular disability with the student, but of inept instruction of basic skills in the classroom.

Such programs allow for withdrawal of students during the school day to be given additional instruction. These include special classrooms for some children whose problems are not sufficiently addressed by withdrawal programs. The decision for such special placement is usually based on the diagnosis of the school psychometrist or psychologist at an additional cost. Further expenses develop out of the support services for such programs, everything from teachers' aides to special equipment, additional transportation, professional services of educational and medical consultants, and extra materials. Again, this failure to get it done right the first time adds huge expenditures to the budgets of each school district.

We also have to add in the administrative costs of these programs at the local, state/provincial and federal levels of government. Everything from record-keeping to managing the grants from other levels of government to policy-making is required. Further, the money allocated to research and its dissemination through conferences, forums and other types of meetings adds yet more to these already sizable costs.

Most parents and taxpayers would probably be willing to bite the bullet and pay the piper if they could be assured that literacy and numeracy would be accomplished by the end of the elementary school years. But 85% of children in elementary schools who are enrolled in special education programs show no change at the end of the program as measured by standardized tests (Carnine, personal communication).

Academic Remediation at the Secondary School Level

As a result, special education classes to teach reading, writing and arithmetic proliferate in the secondary schools as well. They have about the same level of success as in the elementary panel and in many cases become dumping grounds for students who are discipline problems and/or who perform poorly in the regular secondary classes. The number of students enrolled in special education classes declines dramatically in the upper secondary school grades, largely as a result of students dropping out or being removed from the school by the court system or the school administration. These individuals remain largely illiterate, but are no longer in school. They are still with us and many will require various social services for the remainder of their lives.

College Level Literacy Courses

Sadly, the need for remedial-education classes does not end there. In Ontario, each of the twenty-two community colleges have remedial reading and writing programs for students who cannot pass their Basic English course or their Basic English examination. At Seneca College, one of the earliest community colleges to recognize the problem and set up such programs, 30% to 40% of first year students are expected to enroll in remedial English courses.

The lack of adequate college preparation has resulted in an increase in failure rates in three-year community college courses, rising from 10% to 50% over the 30 years of the colleges' existence.

Each of these programs requires the same kinds of resources as the ones initially set up in the elementary schools. There is also the additional cost of tuition, student loans, housing and all the other expenses related to higher education.

Despite these assists, a Council of Ministers survey indicates that 11% of college graduates are functionally illiterate (Cairns, 1988).

It is much the same in American higher education settings. Many of the community colleges in the United States have similar extra educational services for illiterate and underprepared students.

University Level Remediation

Even the universities across North America have seen the need to offer remedial English and Math classes to first-year students. Some of these programs have developed from student tutoring programs into full-time, on-campus learning centers. Perhaps the most notable of these, in terms of its success and its research contributions, is the Center for Individual Studies at Jacksonville State University in Jacksonville, Alabama, administered since its inception by Dr. Claudia McDade.

In its twenty-year history, it has assisted 35% of the undergraduates of the university by tracking their progress and ensuring their success with empirically-based remedial and tutorial programs across a variety of courses. Despite its undisputed benefits and the eventual cost savings it may yield to the university, not to mention the students, it still requires a budget of almost $300,000 per year.

Not many programs can boast of such results. Unfortunately the initial low level of proficiency is seen again as Cairns (1988) indicates that 8% of Canadian university graduates are illiterate.

Adult Education

The direct cost of having to provide continuous remediation from kindergarten through university to keep students from failing or "dropping out" is perhaps the easiest to define. There are other less easily determined costs relating to the provision of educational services to individuals who leave school before graduation.

Most school boards and many colleges have, in the past, provided adult education either as a full-time day program, night school, distance education or some variation of these to help adults learn literacy skills and to earn credits toward a secondary school diploma. Typically these programs involve two to five full-time teachers, some aides, a secretary or office manager and all of the other costs related to providing instruction.

The After-School Tutorial Business

Another cost is found in the extra assistance paid for directly by parents when they cannot get adequate help from their school. At last count, Canada had over 500 different tutorial companies offering such services. There are many more retired teachers, who, like music teachers, tutor a few children each year in their homes to top up their pensions. Several large companies, such as Sylvan Learning Centers of Seattle, have franchised internationally and have several hundred centers spread across the continent. The private remedial education market can be a lucrative enterprise. It adds yet more costs to the fight to make our students capable of surviving and succeeding at school and beyond.

Illiteracy and Employability

Illiterate people are less employable and more frequently among claimants for unemployment benefits, welfare payments and mother's allowance benefits. Kozol (1986) reports that in the U.S., $6 billion annually is paid in unemployment benefits and child-welfare payments to individuals who do not possess the basic skills to maintain employment.

Even semi-literate employees are an added cost to a company and to the country. There are many cases of errors made by illiterate and semi-literate workers which have resulted in huge costs to their employers.

In 1982, The Center for Public Resources did a national survey in the United States to determine the extent of basic skill deficiencies within corporations. Some results of the survey are reported in Gary McCuen's book, *Illiteracy in America.*

The findings, though not entirely unexpected, paint a bleak picture of what has happened to past graduates of our school systems. The results indicate that in the ranks of half of America's corporations, secretarial employees, skilled laborers, managers, supervisors and accounting staff had writing deficiencies. Frequently, they showed an inability to spell correctly, to punctuate accurately or to use appropriate grammar.

More than half of the companies surveyed indicated that

49

at least a portion of their employees were inadequate in necessary math skills. More than half also complained about the level of the speaking and listening skills their employees possessed. Fully two-thirds of the respondents indicated that these skill deficits interfered with the company's capacity to promote from within.

A similar survey in 1994 of entrepreneurs in Canada by *Financial Post* and Arthur Anderson reveals that 56% of employers do not believe that the school system is providing them with the type of graduate they wish to hire. That result is up from 50% the previous year and up almost 20% over the last five-year period. Businesses chafe about the taxes they are paying and the meager return they are realizing from the billions spent on education.

In September, 1987, *USA Today* estimated an annual cost of $225 billion in lost industrial productivity, unrealized tax revenues, welfare and unemployment payments, crime and prisons.

Illiteracy in the Workplace

Workers' Compensation claims resulting from accidents or injuries of illiterate and semi-literate workers add millions in costs to companies' books each year. The Ontario Workers' Compensation Board has an unsecured liability of $150,000,000 and is being dismantled by the current Progressive Conservative government after eighty years of operation. It processed approximately 300,000 accident and injury claims in each of the past five years. The new agency will make life much more difficult for claimants, especially regarding their opportunity to appeal the agency's decisions.

Other Costs

Insurance claims, repair costs for damage to machinery and lost time as a result of damage or injury also add additional sums to this staggering cost.

Illiterate people who cannot follow medical regimens, who

cannot learn about and use preventative medical practices adequately and who cannot even read the directions on their medication add further to medical costs.

The Human Costs of Illiteracy

While the dollar costs are high, the cost in human terms is much higher and much harder to estimate. Perhaps the greatest cost for the illiterate individual is to be excluded from the main channel of communication upon which our society functions - the written word. The additional personal cost is to be made to feel embarrassed, marginalized and ignorant as a result of not being able to do what others seem to do so easily. In order to hide the stigma of illiteracy, some people are forced to build an elaborate web of deceit. Many develop sophisticated coping strategies to cover their inability to read and write, living every day with the constant threat of discovery.

This exclusion from use of the printed word renders people helpless in many situations. Filling out forms for employment, social assistance, medical and legal assistance is beyond their capability and results in their avoidance of these settings as much as humanly possible.

Even the simple task of selecting groceries can be a nightmare. Many foods are packaged so that you must be able to read in order to see what you are buying. For obvious cost-saving reasons, many brands of soup have uniform packaging except for the written label specifying the contents. Such homogeneity creates additional problems for illiterate shoppers. They have a much more difficult time attempting to do any amount of comparative shopping. If one prefers "low-salt" or "cholesterol-free" products, one reads the ingredients information on the side panels of most packaged foods, an option not available to the non-reading consumer.

The process continues at the checkout counter in trying to make change, in presenting food stamps or seeing that you were charged correctly. It continues again in the kitchen where no recipe book can assist you to make a new dish or vary an old one. Again, the potential embarrassment and fear of discovery prevails through all of these activities.

A Sense of Helplessness

Can you envision, for a moment, standing over your sick infant's crib in the dark wee hours of the morning with a bottle of medicine whose label you cannot read, hoping that you have selected the right one and that you can remember how much to give your child? Such fear and frustration should be unnecessary.

Parents such as these cannot lead by example in helping their children become literate. They are unable to read to them, a factor reported in child-development literature as important to school success. As a result, many illiterate families have few, if any, books of their own. They do not tend to frequent libraries or to expose their children to libraries and their programs.

Once their children do enter school, illiterate parents are less likely to visit the classroom or attend school functions including parent/teacher conferences in which requests for help from home could be made by an unaware teacher. Most teachers would have no way of knowing which of his pupils' parents might be unable to read.

These parents are at a loss to assist their children with their studies. They may be less likely to encourage them to get involved in other school functions such as science fairs which could require support from home.

They may also knowingly or unwittingly transmit the belief that school is not important, not valuable or even necessary. Such attitudes will not be helpful to any child struggling to survive in school.

On the Road

Even such things as holidays are affected by one's inability to read and make use of information to plan a trip. Without maps, directories, travel guides or other written aids, including street and highway signs, travel becomes more onerous. The word "travel" derives from the French noun "travail" meaning "work". This work becomes doubly difficult when you are deprived of the written word, and it may limit the attempts of those individuals who cannot read. Once more, their condition circumscribes their activities and limits their exposure to the rest of the world and its many teachings.

I have had long-distance truck drivers as students in basic literacy classes, learning introductory phonics and beginning words that should have been taught in the primary grades. I marvel at how they could possibly deliver a load of goods whose manifest sheets they could not read, across thousands of miles to some street address they could not decipher, in some town that they could never find on a map, across international borders with incomprehensible custom forms. How they can do this on time and accurately, keeping up a log as they go, is a wonder to me. These men are far from stupid; they are simply illiterate, a completely curable condition.

The Threat to Our Democratic Heritage

Every politician clearly understands that information is power. Exclusion from readily available information due to illiteracy creates a class of followers with the capacity to directly impact the health of any democracy.

Illiterate individuals are limited to TV news bytes, on-the-hour radio news or word-of-mouth summaries as their major sources of information regarding important political and social issues. Their grasp of serious societal problems and the formulation of policies to address them is limited by the lack of information available to them. Such paucity opens the door to simplistic, jingoistic political solutions favored by demagogues and other practitioners of the "Big Lie".

If a dynamic, persuasive leader organized the political power of these ill-informed individuals, got them registered and into the voting booth, democracy as we know it could be seriously compromised.

In the U.S., given the current demographics on illiteracy, such a split would also occur along racial lines, pitting

African-Americans and Hispanics against whites.

The existing paranoia that such an eventuality could occur is undoubtedly a factor in the rise of the white supremacy movement in the 80s and 90s and of its recent anti-government activities. The vast majority of the membership of these supremacist groups are not known for their extensive reading of the classics, except perhaps *Mein Kampf* in the simplified abridged version on audiotape. They are themselves the residue of a school system which failed to teach them critical thinking skills. Much of their fear is that they can no longer compete economically in a country which is ever so slowly expanding opportunity for its visible minorities, thereby threatening their current jobs and their future prospects. Their resulting siege mentality is expressed in organizations like the Michigan Militia, with its automatic weapons, battle fatigues and fertilizer-based bombs.

Intergenerational Illiteracy

Another huge cost results from the effect one generation of illiterates has on the next. Parents who cannot read are unable to assist their children to break the cycle of illiteracy. They are wholly dependent on others, primarily the school system, to do this for them. They have been sorely disappointed for the past several generations.

With Brown vs. the Board of Education and the legally mandated integration of American schools, visible minorities began to think that their children would finally be given an equal opportunity in education. Where this has happened at all, it has happened very slowly.

In both Canada and the U.S., public schools have traditionally been supported from taxes at the local level. If the community's tax base is small, the subsidies to the schools are usually equally small. Since many minority students live in the cities and counties with the lowest tax bases, their schools receive significantly less money than schools from more affluent areas. The result is larger classes, fewer materials, more poorly paid teachers and poorer results for most, if not all of the children. This continued lack of results at school allows the cycle to remain unbroken and passes to the next generation.

With a "new chance" in integrated schools showing few results, people began to posit other causes for school failure among children of low socio-economic groups. Though varied and exhaustive, none except the federal Office of Education's Follow Through study has provided a clear solution for the remediation of children at risk of school failure.

Part Three

· ·

A Solution

Is There Any Solution?

●●●●●●●●●●●●●●●●●●●●●●●●●●●●●●●●●●●●●

"If you're not part of the solution -
you're part of the problem."
- Anon

What Can We Do?

In order to effectively change something, we need a goal and a plan. We need something to change to. One place to begin is to determine the features of schools that work well. There are currently, and always have been, exemplary educational settings in both Canada and the USA. If we could ascertain the shared characteristics that make these schools exceptional, we could use their philosophies and practices to build a model of a successful school. To the extent that these characteristics are able to be generalized to all schools, we have a starting point for change. A comparison between components of successful schools and the status quo would define the differences and highlight the necessary changes.

Research on Exemplary Schools

There is a significant body of research literature that delineates the key attributes of exemplary schools. Perhaps the best Canadian study was published in 1988 in the *Canadian Journal of Education* by Brock University professor, Patrick O'Neill. O'Neill examined almost 200 studies of critical variables in effective classrooms in the educational research literature. He isolated a set of seventeen factors which contributed to producing excellence. The most significant factor was the quality of the instruction, especially in regard to its clarity. Other factors of importance were the behavioral management of the classroom, teacher expectations of performance and behavior, immediate feedback and the amount of time spent on task.

In their 1993 video, *Failing Grades*, Professor Mark Holmes and Dr. Joe Freedman report six characteristics of effective schools. They have high expectations of academic work and of appropriate classroom behavior. They demonstrate strong instructional efforts and provide a regular assessment of results. The school environment is orderly and pleasant, and there are consistent efforts by the home and school to achieve optimal results.

As a result of surveying the research, we have at least some notion of what is required if we are to be effective. Let's look at some of these factors a little more closely.

The Underlying Philosophy of Current North American Education

In his latest book, *The Schools We Need and Why We Don't Have Them*, E.D. Hirsch very adroitly puts his finger on the major reason for North American school failure. He attributes it to the current philosophy of learning that has permeated classrooms across North America for the past 50 years. It is generally known as the "Progressive Model of Education" and is part of the American Romanticist philosophy espoused by writers and philosophers like Thoreau and Emerson. When misapplied to education, it has led to the disastrous international test results and the growing illiteracy and incompetence today's schools are producing. According to this philosophy, anything that is "unnatural", such as confining children to desks in rows, is inherently bad; anything demanding stressful effort or tedious practice is to be avoided, as it is not immediately rewarding for the child and decimates his natural curiosity.

The application of this naturalistic, discovery-oriented approach became dominant in the early decades of the 20th century. It gained prominence because it effectively polarized the thinking of Americans about educational practices by the language used to describe the major philosophies of the day. Opponents were labeled "conservative" as opposed to "progressive". Their methods were characterized as traditional, teacher-directed, lockstep, boring, repetitive, and failing to teach the "whole" child. Progressive educators, on the other hand, were seen as modern, hands-on, integrated, interesting, individualized and developing the entire child.

The curriculum, objectives and practices emanating from this philosophy are difficult to attack because they are nebulous and non-specific. Being opposed to formal, rigorous skill testing, they provide little, if any, data-based information to determine their efficacy or their failings. Testing, setting objectively measurable standards and structure were among the casualties of this new approach. The reliance on empirical data and replicated results of applied research have little place in the "Romanticist" philosophy of education.

Like the oppressors of leading-edge thinkers like Socrates, Galileo, Semmelwiess and countless others who attempted to place scientific data ahead of beliefs, they feel they already have their answer and would prefer not to be obstructed by facts and demonstrated results. Like the high priests who persecuted Galileo, they are powerful enough to be able to threaten, undermine and forestall the development of any scientific approach to the problem.

The characteristics embodied by Romanticist schools are quite dissimilar to the ones found to be successful by Freedman and Holmes and by O'Neill. Their studies demonstrated that clarity of presentation, structure, corrective feedback and repetition were critical variables in skill development. These characteristics have been increasingly ignored in current educational practices and are reflected in the differences in scores between North American students and those from other nations who advocate more stringent instructional methods.

Effective Instruction - The Research

If we are now convinced that our education system is in

need of a major overhaul, we have to find out more about each of these characteristics and build the best examples of each into a consistent whole.

Especially in terms of instruction, we would have to determine what works, and having done that, we would need to devise a plan and implement it. So the first and most important question then becomes, "What methodologies exist that can clearly demonstrate effective change in the level of skills in our students, particularly those at risk of school failure?"

Background to the Origins of the Research

In order to understand the present situation in education, we must first take a look at our recent past. The question of what would help children in school came from a wholly unexpected source, far removed from the ivory towers of academia, namely, the racial disturbances of the late sixties. During this period, there were severe race riots in many major U.S. cities. These riots in the Watts district of Los Angeles, in Detroit and Memphis, among others, resulted in the mobilization of the National Guard, tanks in the streets, and numerous dead, wounded and jailed citizens. The violence and unrest had the capacity to develop into a race war unless steps were taken to alleviate the conditions in the black urban slums of America. Especially after the violent deaths of black leaders like Martin Luther King, Malcolm X, Medgar Evans and others, poor blacks were leaderless, without hope and hugely frustrated at not having any part of the American Dream.

Head Start and Follow Through

As with the attempt to resolve most problems, the U.S. government set up a commission. Its purpose was to study race relations and what needed to be done to avoid similar events in the future. Then-President Lyndon Johnson declared "The War on Poverty" and established the Office of Economic Opportunity as the strategic headquarters of the new campaign. When the commission reported back, it gave the kind of recommendations that nearly every government report has concluded regarding almost any problem studied, namely, that there needed to be more funding and more education of impoverished Americans.

Among the initiatives of this war on poverty was the creation of the Head Start program which was to give underprivileged children a "head start" at school by providing preschool programs. The hope was that early intervention and instruction would allow inner-city children to be successful at school, thus breaking the cycle of poverty and enabling them to eventually participate in the mainstream economy of the nation.

Given the serious nature of the problem, Johnson announced a second project which would follow children from Head Start or other similar programs through their primary years at school. It suggested tracking 190,000 children through the first three grades of elementary school, trying to prevent academic failure by building solid skills. Project Follow Through was born as a responsibility of the federal Office of Education and was to cost $120,000,000.

There is lack of agreement as to what, if any, part the results from the Head Start program played in the formation of the Follow Through project. The best analysis available (Watkins, 1997) suggests that any decision regarding Follow Through was more driven by political expedience than by research results, and that any results which might have been available were highly suspect in terms of their research methodologies, data-collection procedures and use of the data as a basis for conclusions.

The Plan

According to Watkins, the original Follow Through plan was to be implemented nationally, but because of budget cutbacks it was scaled down to become a research project with thirty demonstration sites in the first year. As a justification for the program, planned variation of the curriculum to be used in the experiment was one of the features of the project. It appears that the design of the research may never have been to determine effective instructional procedures as much as it was a means to expand the Follow Through program to more sites.

Nonetheless, the first step was to contact all of the universities, foundations and agencies conducting research on instructional methods which might have been interested in participating in such a project. They were essentially invited to submit proposals outlining their "solutions". Eighteen different groups representing the entire spectrum of educational pedagogies responded to the request. Sixteen of these became sponsors.

The Office of Education then wrote to every single school district in the nation and invited them to become involved. They feared that many poorly funded boards might not be interested in the project, especially if it cost them resources or time. In order to interest these districts, the Office of Education offered a number of enticements. Since this project was being run as research, each school chosen would have a control group classroom for every experimental group in their district. Each of these would receive most or all of the same benefits that the experimental classroom was granted.

A teacher would be provided for each group of 25 students enrolled in the study. There would also be one aide assigned for every eight children. A consultant would be provided to train staff and monitor the program for one week each month. And in case that wasn't enough, an annual cash grant of $750.00 per student for the three years of the study was offered.

Since this affected both the control group and the experimental group, it added up to a significant amount of money. Not surprisingly, applicants for the Follow Through study were in abundance.

Flawed Design

The Follow Through sponsors met with the prospective school districts and made a brief presentation outlining their model and its philosophy and practices. The school districts then selected the model that they felt best matched their schools' goals. This lack of random distribution of methods across sponsors did not meet the stipulation of acceptable research design, a not uncommon fate of applied social research.

The Office of Education also hired an external evaluator, first Stanford Research Institute and later, Abt Associates of Cambridge. They were to set up, monitor and report on the project so that the Office of Education remained as an unbiased third party. Abt Associates sat down with the sixteen sponsors and agreed as to what constituted success and how it should be measured. They tested all of the children at the beginning and end of each school year. They collected, tabulated and analyzed the data and wrote the final report for the Director of the Office of Education.

The Results

At the end of the three-year study, only two of sixteen models showed consistent academic gains for children at risk of school failure. Children in some models, such as the Bank Street "Discovery Learning", did not even do as well as children in the control group.

Of the two methods which were successful, the Direct Instruction model from the University of Oregon accounted for the largest share of the variance in the data. The second model, Behavior Analysis from the University of Kansas, accounted for much of the remainder. Both prototypes were behavioral in orientation. They also ranked first and second on affective measures, that is to say, how the children felt about their involvement and their learning.

As Engelmann (1992) points out in his book, *War Against The Schools' Academic Child Abuse*, Direct Instruction was:

• first in reading
• first in arithmetic
• first in spelling
• first in language

•first in basic skills
•first in academic cognitive skills
•first in positive self-image

When the research was concluded and clear results emerged from the data, it was time to move. However, the government did not act on any of the results by implementing the successful models across the nation. They simply declared the entire experiment a success.

"Facts do not cease to exist because they are ignored." - Aldous Huxley

Having declared the project successful, the government continued to fund any and all models, regardless of their proven effectiveness or lack thereof. At the end of the second three-year cycle, another final report was submitted to the Director of the Office of Education. It showed essentially the same outcome in the data as the initial report. In fact, overlaying the charts from the original study and those from the replication study reveals almost no discrepancies.

The Idiocy

It is incomprehensible that The Office of Education has never shown any real interest in whether or not one particular method helps disadvantaged kids more than any other. It certainly was not interested in being seen to promote one method over another. That would have created a new and different kind of political problem - telling teachers what and how to teach. Since only two methods showed positive results, and since those were the only two behavioral programs involved in Follow Through, the Office of Education could have been seen as endorsing a particular technology, theory or school of thought. They could have been seen to be infringing on the teachers' professionalism by dictating methodology, something for which the powerful teacher associations would hardly sit still.

The fact that many publishers would have suddenly found their special education materials excluded as ineffective was another consideration. The sum total of these concerns led to a rather bizarre decision. . . to replicate the entire study yet again!

At the time of this writing, the Follow Through project is in its seventh or eighth replication. Most of the copies of the original studies were shredded during the Reagan administration.

The Final Insult

The federal Office of Education also manages the National Diffusion Network, a program which identifies and disseminates "exemplary" instructional programs on a national basis. Each of the original Follow Through programs is listed as being worthy of national distribution as an exemplary program, despite the data. The credibility of the Follow Through results is further eroded by decisions such as these. It also does little to lend credence to the reputation of the Office of Education.

Precision Teaching - Another Effective Method

There have been other successful interventions using educational technologies in schools that have been reported in the educational research literature over the years. Some include strong empirical data to substantiate their effectiveness. One such research initiative was the Sacajawea Project in the early seventies in Montana.

In this project, elementary school students spent part of each day practicing basic skills in reading, math, spelling and writing. They recorded their scores on timed samples of their performances. Usually the timing would be for a period of one minute, and the score would be noted on a Standard Celeration Chart each day. The project began as research (Beck and Clement, 1976) and was implemented in schools across the state of Montana during a twelve-year period.

By the third year of the program, students in the Sacajawea Project achieved scores 25 percentile points higher than control-group students on the Iowa Test of Basic Skills. These increases in reading were dramatic, but they were eclipsed by a 44 percentile difference in math scores.

Clearly the use of Precision Teaching techniques made a substantive difference in the skills of the children for whom they were provided. But again, despite their effectiveness, the methods were not adopted by school districts, and the project eventually ended. It is important to understand what works. It is equally important to determine why effective methods are not immediately seized upon by our schools when those methods can clearly show academic benefits for all kinds of students. Some argue that it is a question of money.

A Question of Money

Even when school boards are made aware of what works they almost always ignore it. Universally, the reason given is that they do not have the funds for such remedial programs. Many of the explanations given by school administrators are blown out of the water by recent research. Coleman and LaRocque (1991) in their book, *Struggling to be Good Enough*, report that there is little, if any, relationship between the amount of money spent and the effectiveness of the schooling. They found that profligate school boards tended to have lower records of performance. They explain their findings as bad school districts trying to manage their problems with increasing emphasis on non-teaching, administrative staff trying to purchase quality as if it were a commodity, whereas more frugal schools spend their money to more directly assist their teaching staff.

Coleman and LaRocque point out six characteristics of "good" school boards:

1. They focus on instruction.
2. They encourage the monitoring of progress with informal and formal tests on a regular basis.

3. They change specific practices when they don't get the
   results that teachers, parents and students expect.
4. They have a commitment to excellence.
5. They report results to parents on a regular basis.
6. They actively seek parental feedback and input.

Academic Child Abuse

Barbara Bateman makes the case that to ignore helpful
methods is tantamount to abusing the child. It is a form of
neglect. She termed the situation where ineffective teachers
put children at risk of school failure as a result of their own
ineptitude as "academic child abuse".

Summary

• The results of Project Follow Through were never implemented as a national remedial educational initiative in the
  War Against Poverty. It became entrapped in a bureaucrat-
  ic morass and made no significant impact on the academic
  skills of the children it was meant to serve. However, it did
  attain one goal. It clearly delineated those technologies
  which did and did not work for children at risk of school
  failure. It pointed out decisively that the Direct Instruction
  and Behavior Modification models were superior in basic
  skills, both in cognitive skills and in affective measures in
  helping to erase the learning gap between socio-economi-
  cally deprived children and their middle-class peers. The
  child-centered, self-discovery, "romantic" models failed mis-
  erably on every one of these measures. While Follow
  Through was a flawed social experiment driven more by
  political necessity and expedience than by the need to discern effective remedial and preventative methods, it
  remains the best data available, whatever its shortcomings.
  Although the results must be interpreted with reserve, it is
  still our best guess as to what works for children at risk of
  school failure..
• Despite clear and unequivocal results showing marked gains

in academic performance over a twelve-year period, Precision Teaching methods used in the Sacajawea Project have not been widely adopted by public schools. Given the crisis which schools face, one would expect that school administrators would flock to any technology which could demonstrate an ability to reduce or eradicate literacy and numeracy problems. This has not historically been the case and it remains so today.

- Money, or the lack of it, is an insufficient explanation for what is not happening to produce school excellence. In fact, it may be a detriment if it is used to overmanage the functions of the classroom. High standards of learning are achieved by the efforts of parents and teachers to work out sensible strategies and solutions cooperatively.

- The best solution is to adopt and integrate those methods which can empirically demonstrate their effectiveness to provide the materials, the training, the leadership and the commitment towards quality education. It is also critical to monitor the implementation and use of any adopted technology for the benefits of the children, their families and the society at large. When we give schools the tools, we should expect them to finish the job. If they choose not to use these effective tools, we should develop options for the benefit of the students, even if that means abandoning the current schools and their ineffective methods.

A Model for
Effective Teaching

• •

"If at first you don't succeed, try another method."
- Anon

The Model

In order to effectively teach anyone anything, there are a number of conditions to be set in place. First, you must have an objective or goal as to what you want teachers to teach or students to learn. Secondly, you must have the necessary degree of order and organization. No one teaches or learns well in the midst of chaos. Thirdly, you need a method of instruction that actually works. If the student didn't learn, the teacher didn't teach. Next, you need some accurate and dependable form of measurement so that you can see the difference before and after instruction and/or practice. And finally, you need to provide practice until the new skill is well learned. This includes two types. The beginning stages are generally directed by the teacher and monitored to avoid unnecessary errors and to speed up learning. Once a sufficient level of skill has been achieved, the learners can begin to practice more independently until they reach fluent levels of performance.

All of this may sound easy and straightforward, but in reality it flies in the face of what actually happens in most classrooms, most of the time. In the majority of current educational settings, at least one of the components is either missing or so poorly implemented as to leave students at risk of academic failure.

As a simple pie chart, first presented as an overview in a workshop by Eric Haughton, the model looks something like this:

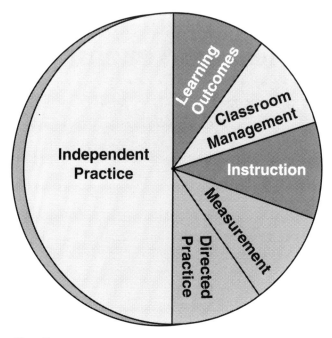

The Six Components of the QLC Model

The relative size of each component indicated on the pie chart pretty much corresponds to the total amount of time dedicated to it. Practice takes by far the lion's share of the time, up to 60%, and independent effort is the largest component of practice, almost 50% of the total time involved.

The Quinte Learning Center methods emanated from the early drawing that Eric used and from our subsequent work together. Once we opened the center, we attached particular technologies to some of the components and instituted the complete model in our classrooms beginning in 1979. Parts of the system had been used by some teachers in the Hastings County Board while Eric and I were there. The complete model as a method to run a classroom or a school did not occur until the Quinte Learning Center opened its doors. The integration involved bringing students under instructional control using behavior analytic procedures, teaching concepts and operations using Direct Instruction programs and measuring progress using Precision Teaching techniques. It also involved giving sufficient practice using Direct Instruction student materials and specially designed practice materials similar to those in the Sacajawea project.

A refinement of the original pie chart, the QLC model looks like this:

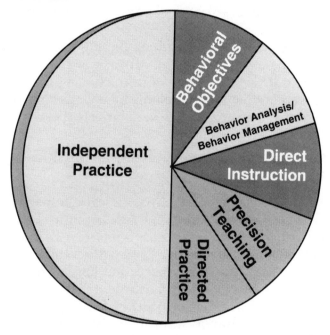

1) Setting Objectives - Learning Outcomes

The setting of objectives as part of the model resulted from a Learning Outcomes Initiative by Hastings County which was being implemented just as we joined our support teams. The Learning Outcomes program attempted to list and describe the various results to be expected of any particular curriculum at each grade level. The Hastings County Board invested a great deal of time, money and energy to create this program which eventually covered the curriculum from kindergarten to the end of secondary school.

This method of mapping out objectives to guide teachers is very useful, especially if they are not using cohesive programs which already incorporate learning outcomes. Fortunately, Direct Instruction, our instructional technology of choice, already includes a complete analysis of the necessary objectives for each subject area at each level. The Direct Instruction programs also go one step further by outlining the scope of the objectives in each program and arranging the outcomes in a sequence which would create the most effective instructional approach.

The common failure of learning objectives programs is that they become a laundry list of outcomes with little or no measurement, little or no order of instructional presentation and no consistent method of holding schools accountable to reach the stated objectives. They soon become shelfware.

2) Managing the Classroom - Behavior Analysis and Behavior Management

The second segment of the chart deals with managing the behavior of the students inside and outside of the classroom. The psychological research literature is replete with studies of applied classroom management. There are several excellent books on the topic, including Becker and Engelmann's *Contingency Management of Classroom Behavior* (1976).

The behavior management model by Don Bushell (1974) at the University of Kansas was part of the Follow Through study and was second only to Direct Instruction in producing superior results.

3) Effective Teaching - Direct Instruction

The third slice of the pie relates to the actual teaching of the curriculum each day in the classroom to produce learning. Because of its exemplary results in Follow Through and our success in the classrooms of Hastings County, Direct Instruction is the obvious instructional method in our integrated model. It provides a host of field-tested, off-the-shelf programs to cover the essential elementary school core curriculum in reading, reading comprehension, spelling, writing and math, American history and some science.

4) Measuring Achievement - Precision Teaching

The addition of Precision Teaching as the measurement component provides us with the ability to gather data quickly and accurately and make decisions immediately. It allows the student to become an active participant and decision-maker in directing his own learning. It provides a comparative learning history of each student, each class, or of an entire school over days, weeks, months and years of work on specific tasks. This historical record is an invaluable tool for determining the effectiveness of instruction, practice and the curriculum decisions of teachers and/or students. This element, especially when coupled with the efficiency of Direct Instruction methods, creates the synergy which powers the new amalgamation.

Most of the settings using some form of the basic QLC model also utilize standardized educational tests as part of their evaluation strategy. Such instruments as the Iowa Test of Basic Skills, the Canadian Test of Basic Skills, the Wide Range Achievement Test or others are administered at the beginning and end of the school year. These standardized tests are administered mostly for the benefit of those educational professionals who rely on such tests in their placement decisions for students returning to public schools. None of the founders places much stock in the results of these standardized test scores, but since they are the common currency of contemporary education, and since we have a responsibility to our students, we do report them to schools. A student's set of daily-charted data showing fluent performances on a precise task is a much more solid tool for analysis and decision-making.

5) Directed Practice

6) Independent Practice

The largest single piece of the pie is the practice component comprising more than half of the available time. Of the two types, directed practice under the watchful eye of the teacher is smaller but of greater importance. It functions as the quality assurance process. Once the teacher and the learner are confident that the student's attempts will result in stronger learning, it can be given over to independent practice. The change to independent practice promotes the fluency-building requirements of the model.

A Better Mouse Trap

Taken together, the components of this model produce better learning at a faster rate than any other system around, including the individual parts themselves. The synergy created by this integration places an enormously powerful array of teaching tools in any instructor's hands. It is capable of wiping out illiteracy in any English-speaking nation, especially if it is competently implemented into our public schools in the beginning elementary grades. An in-depth examination of each of the model's six components is found in Part 4.

Part Four

. . . .

An Effective Model for Academic Excellence ~ The Components of the QLC Model

Behavioral Objectives / Learning Outcomes

"I care not what subject is taught if only it be taught well."
- T.H. Huxley

What are they?

Behavioral objectives, also known as learning outcomes, are the expected products of instruction. They are the skills you intend the student to possess once the teaching and practice have been completed. They are not simply lesson plans. They are a completely defined, overall design of the skills a particular program expects to impart to the learner. They are best summarized in a scope and sequence chart.

A major tenet in creating objectives is that the objectives are attainable by all of the students given proper placement, sufficient and effective instruction followed by adequate practice. Objectives do not change as a function of the learner. The starting point and amount of effort to attain the objectives might vary, but not the outcomes themselves.

Scope and Sequence

The scope and sequence of any curriculum lay out the range of skills the program teaches and the order in which they will be taught. Scope and sequence force the program creator to decide exactly what will be included in a particular program or component of a program series, and what will be excluded as unnecessary or inappropriate.

Once the scope of the skills to be taught has been decided upon, it becomes possible to begin to sequence them so that they are most economically and efficiently taught. This part requires great skill in an instructional designer. Some skills require more time and more frequent practice across lessons. Some subskills must be taught before others so that the student is never asked to do a task for which all of the necessary preskills have not been previously taught . A major difference among instructional programs in all subject areas across the curriculum lies in the degree to which the authors have paid attention to the appropriate sequencing of the skills to be taught in each part of each lesson of the program.

To the extent that this issue has not been specifically addressed, the program is likely to contain instructional design flaws. While some students who come to the task with a host of previous skills may not be dramatically affected by poorly defined skill sequences, weaker students can be academically annihilated by such oversights.

Teachers are often unaware of the design of the scope and sequences of skills in the programs they are asked to deliver. Many programs do not explicitly outline them in any of the materials provided. Teachers, despite their training, are generally not given specific courses in instructional design. If asked, few teachers could systematically outline the scope of the skills their current reading program is intended to teach, the order in which skills and subskills would be taught and the map by which they could ensure that each student would, in fact, learn each of the skills listed.

Until teacher-training institutions ensure that every teacher is either trained or retrained in this level of instructional design, it is unfair to hold the teacher accountable for instructional design considerations in program selection. That responsibility falls to the person who is selecting the textbooks, programs and training from which the teacher is expected to deliver instruction in a given subject. Frequently, teachers have little input into these decisions which are handed down from on high by people who haven't been in a classroom in a donkey's years.

No one expects jet pilots to build their own planes, or even to maintain them. They are asked to do a pre-flight check to determine any obvious deficiencies in the craft before they take off. Teachers, however, are asked to build their lessons as well as teach them, but they are no better equipped to do so than the jet pilot is to maintain an airplane. It is enough to ask teachers to deliver a properly designed program so that their students become skillful. This task, given its accompanying monitoring, practice, corrections and marking, requires all of the energy and skill of even the most dedicated instructor. In teaching, like housework, there is always more to be done. Expecting teachers to also create the tools needed for effective instruction is to invite production of inferior lessons and increased chance of failure, especially for students at risk.

A Word About Instructional Design

Instructional design is not a feature to be taken lightly. Just to draw up the learning outcomes presupposes a great deal of knowledge about how they will be organized, what will and will not be included, how much instruction and review will be required, and where it will occur and recur across all of the lessons of a particular subject.

There are relatively few people who are skillful in this aspect of curriculum development. Such instructional design specialists are typically not in control of editing the final production of the reading series materials of major educational publishers. Those decisions are much more driven by whether or not the program satisfies the lists of criteria set down by the textbook approval committees of the major states in the U.S. market without whose sanction the production of the program is not a financially viable undertaking.

In attempting to satisfy the varying curriculum demands of the top ten textbook-approval committees, any book could soon become so large as to be inordinately expensive to produce, let alone buy as classroom materials. The most commonly used strategy to accommodate the reviewers is to foreshorten much of the material into review exercises so that this humongous load of objectives is nominally included in a reasonable number of pages.

Such unintended constraints placed on publishers by state textbook-approval committees put thoughtful instructional design at great risk of being sacrificed to the exigencies of meeting somewhat arbitrary standards set by these well-meaning but misdirected authorities. It is a major reason why better textbooks are not available in North American classrooms today.

Behavior Analysis / Behavior Management

• •

"The love of praise, howe'er concealed by art,
Reigns more or less, and glows in ev'ry heart."
- Edward Young

A Simple Premise

For many years, man has studied man in an effort to describe what he does and why he does it. A variety of theories has been promulgated to explain his essence and his actions. Some theorists like Sigmund Freud believed that man was largely driven by unconscious forces and that his behavior or the lack of it could be attributed to the effects of these warring unconscious forces within him. Many of these were considered by Freud to be sexual drives censured by society.

Others, like the philosopher Jean-Jacques Rousseau, have seen man as a blank sheet, a *tabula rasa*, on which society carves its influences and gradually socializes and even corrupts his innocent nature and beauty. Still others see man as determined by his genetic makeup and programmed to become whatever he is by the biological determinants of his species.

Behaviorists look at the observable behavior of the human as a legitimate starting point of study. They tend not to postulate other hidden, difficult-to-analyze influences as the *raison d'être* for man's behavior. The study of the behavior itself is seen as a worthwhile goal of science. Many other philosophers and social scientists have scoffed at this behavioral approach as shallow or mechanistic. The argument as to the value of attempting to understand the nature of man by behavioral or other means is well beyond the purpose of this book.

But the study of behavior, as researched by B.F. Skinner and his colleagues, has provided us with a set of principles and practices that are useful in applied situations. Understanding the principles and practices of applied behavior analysis helps a teacher to be in much better control of the teaching environment and thus better able to deliver effective instruction. The process is one of managing the performance of the learner.

A Brief History

Behavior Analysis and Behavior Modification are the applied components of learning theory, a set of doctrines outlined by Skinner, Pavlov, Thorndike, J.B. Watson and a host of other theorists who developed classical and operant conditioning.

A large number of concepts including reward, punishment and modeling are found in behavior analysis. Out of these and others evolved a significant body of research and practices for understanding and altering human behavior. Many of these theoretical constructs and applied practices were first developed in animal laboratories and then applied to other situations, including classrooms. As a result, there exists a large body of current research available to solve management problems in schools and similar institutions.

Learning

In behavioral terms, learning is a process by which experiences or practices result in a relatively permanent change in behavior. We cannot measure the learning, but we can measure the performance as an index of learning. Learning to play the guitar is a relatively permanent change in behavior which can be easily measured by hearing the learner play.

Classical Conditioning

Ivan Pavlov started out in 1910 studying the intestinal secretions of animals in an attempt to better understand the

role of salivation in digestion. He noticed that the dogs salivated when they were given food powder. Pavlov understood
this phenomenon as a natural occurrence. He also noticed
that the dogs began to salivate just before they were actually
given the food and he became interested in that observation.
To study this phenomenon, Pavlov conducted what became
the classic study in learning theory. He rang a bell and simultaneously presented food powder to the dog. At the sight of
the food the dog salivated. After pairing the presentation of
food with the sound of the bell on many successive trials,
Pavlov rang the bell without presenting the food powder, and
the dog salivated. Since dogs don't normally salivate at the
sound of a bell, Pavlov concluded that the dog had been con-
ditioned to salivate. The dog continued to salivate at the sound
of the bell in the absence of food for many trials and eventually ceased.

What Pavlov serendipitously discovered has parallels in
human behavior. Humans learn to respond to sounds that signal danger, such as fire alarms, smoke alarms, sirens, etc. These
sounds have been paired with images or events that are harmful or potentially dangerous, such as fire. When we cross on
green lights and wait at red lights we display further evidence
of conditioning.

Operant Conditioning

In classical conditioning, the behavior is elicited by some
specific stimulus and we learn to transfer the response to some
previously neutral stimulus. In operant conditioning, the
behavior is emitted by the subject voluntarily, rather than trig-
gered by outside events. A student raising his hand in class to
get the teacher's attention is an example of operant conditioning. The behavior is designed to operate on the environment in a way that will bring some kind of satisfaction to the
individual.

Much of what we know about the principles of operant
conditioning were first described by B.F. Skinner. The bulk of
his laboratory research was done in what became known as
"Skinner boxes". The Skinner box contained a lever which

protruded through the wall just above a cup into which food pellets fell when the bar was pressed by the experimental animal.

Acquisition

"An animal psychologist is a man who pulls habits out of rats."
- Anon

In operant conditioning, correct responses or approximations to correct responses are rewarded. Incorrect responses are ignored or even punished. In the original studies, when the animal approached the bar, a food pellet dropped into the cup or food magazine. If the animal made a second approach, another pellet dropped. This process was repeated until the animal associated moving toward the bar with getting food. As it sniffed to find more food, any movement of the animal's head or paw in the direction of the bar above the food cup was rewarded, any movement away from the bar was not. Soon the animal increased time and effort spent close to the lever. As the animal explored for more food, touching the bar resulted in reward. Touching the bar gradually escalated into pressing on the bar. Now the animal was "learning" how to produce the food pellets by emitting the appropriate response.

Acquisition is achieved through shaping the behavior by rewarding successively closer approximations to the desired response using trial and error.

The same techniques are used by astute animal trainers to teach "tricks" to dolphins, to break horses and teach them dressage, and to train the family dog. Some species are more trainable than others. Monkeys and rats are easily trained; cats, for example, are more difficult subjects.

Verbal Instruction and Modeling

When language can be used in teaching and training, explaining what is to be done is an important way of helping people learn new responses or to change old behavior. Instructions to children to "work quickly and quietly", or to adults to "use the rule to solve this problem" cut down on the trial and error responses that may result when language cannot initially be used. Pairing language and rewards also allows the trainer to bring the subject under verbal control after the behavior has been learned. "Fetch", "Sit", "Lie Down", "Play Dead" are all examples of verbal cueing of behavior that results in a response or a series of responses that will be rewarded.

Showing someone how to do something by demonstrating it can also be an efficient method of learning. The demonstration can be analyzed into clear steps and modeled with a verbal explanation. The coaching of sports involves a lot of modeling and explanation.

Reinforcement

Once the behavior has been produced, reinforcement increases the probability that it will be produced again. Pigeons who are randomly fed grains of wheat often engage in the behavior which immediately preceded the appearance of the grain, such as flapping their wings or turning in circles. This process of accidentally reinforcing behaviors is called superstitious conditioning. Sports fans often see the same type of superstitious behavior in games. For example, before a foul shot or before stepping into the batter's box, players go through some ritualistic behavior which they associate with "luck" or increasing their chances of success.

Some people let superstitious behavior become an important part of their lives. For them, a behavior that at some time was accidentally rewarded has been strengthened by being reinforced often enough to become a strong and repetitive response. Such behaviors in the extreme can become ritualistic and confining. So far this hasn't happened to me - touch wood!

Reinforcement strengthens behavior even when the learner doesn't know that he is being reinforced. When students in one study were asked to name things and were reinforced with nods for giving plural nouns, they named significantly more of them, although they could not explain why they might have done so and were unaware of being reinforced.

There are two kinds of reinforcers - positive and negative. Following a response with an outcome which is desirable to the learner is an example of positive reinforcement. Praise, being done, getting a good mark, feeling satisfied with your performance are positively reinforcing. Negative reinforcement ends a difficult or unpleasant situation. Finishing a hard term paper that has kept you up all night, shutting off an alarm clock that has just wakened you from a sound sleep are examples of negative reinforcement. Negative reinforcement is very different than punishment.

Punishment

Punishment consists of something unpleasant happening in order to change or terminate an unacceptable behavior. Punishment can be either the introduction of some aversive condition or the withdrawal of some reinforcer. Getting hit in the face with pepper spray is the application of a noxious stimulus. Adults sometimes resort to hitting or shaking children as a punisher to get them to stop some behavior.

Generally, punishers are to be avoided for a number of reasons. In the first place, organisms of all types adapt to punishers. To maintain their effectiveness, punishers generally have to be increased over time to get the same effect. Parents who physically hit children have in some cases become child batterers because they continually escalate the level of punishment each time the child fails to comply. Punishment also has dangerous side effects in that it often breeds fear and suspicion and undermines trust. People tend to avoid individuals and situations which they find punishing. It's more difficult to raise or teach a child who is fearful or resentful of your previous behavior.

Punishment may also work only while the punisher is around. Once the punisher is absent, the behavior may revert to its former frequency and intensity.

Another form of punishment is the removal of something valued by the individual or group. Having your license taken away for driving under the influence is punishing. Being locked in jail and losing your freedom is punishing. Most societies haphazardly utilize these types of punishers in their court and justice systems. Unfortunately, the inconsistency, variability and delay between the behavior and any punishment undermine their effectiveness dramatically. The reality of life inside prisons is generally a good example of how attempting to change behavior through punishment can go horrendously wrong.

In much better controlled settings, such as in properly designed and implemented behavior management programs, the immediate loss of tokens, points or activities for unacceptable behavior is usually punishing to the learner and results in the reduction of frequency of those behaviors. Removal of reward or the chance for reward is used to reduce unacceptable behavior. Withholding reinforcement is generally used sparingly. Concentrated effort is paid to strengthening more acceptable behavior, rather than punishing unacceptable ones.

The Great Smartie Snatch

One summer, while teaching a group of Grade 1 children a beginning reading program, I used Smarties as a reward for good work. All of the children had a styrofoam cup in front of them into which I dropped the candies when they were trying their best. One student, whom I had placed right in front of me, was very inattentive. He was labeled hyperactive and couldn't read. He would often stare off elsewhere when he was to be looking at the book. I would give the child next to him a Smartie and compliment him for paying attention to the work being presented. As soon as the distracted student did the same thing, I would reward him as well. On one occasion, he looked away in the middle of trying to read a word. Without saying anything, I simply reached into his cup, took a Smartie and ate it. His eyes got as big as saucers, and they were riveted on the book for the rest of the lesson. He not only never lost another Smartie, he usually earned a few more than most of the other students. He also became a very proficient reader.

Immediacy of Reinforcement

In order to be effective, reinforcers of all types must follow the behavior immediately. To the degree that they are removed in time from the behavior, they are likely to be ineffective. The optimum time for reinforcement is within one-half second of the occurrence of the behavior. When a student says the correct sound for decoding a word, verbal reinforcement needs to follow immediately, not several seconds later when he may be thinking about the next word or worse yet, may have just guessed wrongly at the next sound.

Reinforcers that are out of sync with behavior wind up reinforcing the behavior that immediately preceded it. This is, at best, confusing, and at worst, entirely harmful because the learner may have a response strengthened which may have nothing to do with the objective. It may even be counterproductive. The only alternative, when reinforcement cannot for some reason follow immediately, is to verbally bridge the reinforcer with a specific description of what behaviors are being rewarded, not rewarded or punished.

"Good job, Sarah. You're working quietly. Your group earns a point for extra library time on Friday." Or, " Brad, if you keep making your bed each morning like you did today, we can go to McDonalds for lunch on Saturday."

The Nature of Reinforcement

Reinforcers are only reinforcers when they effect a change in the frequency or strength of a behavior. They do not acquire reinforcement value simply because they have been selected by someone as rewards. Being centered out in a meeting for some noble accomplishment is rewarding to some people but embarrassing and punishing to others. A gold star may gain one child praise and envy from his peers, while another child getting the same gold star is the object of teasing, ridicule and maybe even a good thrashing by the school bully at recess. The reward value does not come stuck on the back of the gold star, but in the environment in which it is given. If the same star can be added to a line of stars that earns a pack of hockey cards or extra recess, it can take on a whole new set of reinforcing properties.

The same thing is true of punishers and negative reinforcers. They change as a function of the needs and desires of the learner. The potency of a reinforcer tends to vary inversely with the frequency of its use. How do you want your fourth filet mignon done? Probably not cooked, maybe frozen. Abused individuals get battered, in part, because the same level of punishment used before is now insufficient to control the behavior.

Teachers should always be aware of the type and schedule of reinforcement they are using with their students. With new learning, the schedule should generally be richer than in later, more established learning.

As the student learns, at least a part of the reward should become embedded in the task. The sense of mastery and competence that one derives from being able to do something which used to be hard or impossible can itself become a reward. Being praised by a mentor or a peer for doing well may become less important than being able to do something independently.

Extinction

Extinction of a response occurs when the behavior consistently goes unrewarded. Gamblers finally walk away from a slot machine even though they still have money. Extinction is often used by teachers to eliminate mildly unacceptable conduct. If attention is a reinforcer for some inappropriate action, the teacher ensures that attention is never given to that particular behavior. If a client wishes to discuss his personal problems during instruction time, a good teacher will place this behavior under extinction by telling the student that he cannot deal with the issue at that time but would be willing to meet after class. Very few ever accept such an offer when it means giving up their own time in lieu of class time. Those who do are usually serious about needing someone to talk to.

Consistency

No reinforcer works if the learner cannot predict which behavior or how much of any given behavior will result in reward. People who give rewards after withholding them until children are totally out of control are unwittingly teaching them that this is the level of whining or tantrums they must reach if they really want this reward. Such inconsistency inadvertently teaches the child to be exhibit inappropriate behavior in a variety of settings. One of the most common instances occurs in the grocery store where management has strategically placed all kinds of tasty treats at various spots, including near the checkout stands. It is a lesson in behavior management to watch different parents deal with their child's requests (demands) for a variety of items. Some are completely consistent in either granting or refusing the plea. Many even give some explanation as to why they are allowing or refusing the child's choice. Others ignore the child, dragging him along with the shopping cart, the child screaming up and down the aisles, before they give in. If the parent says "no" and acts accordingly, the child learns that no amount of whining will change the decision. To the degree that consistency occurs, the learner is in a position to determine the likelihood of being rewarded. The teacher or parent is simply the arbitrator and deliverer of the reward system.

"One of the teacher's constant tasks is to take a roomful of live wires and see that they are grounded." - Anon Teacher

Behavior management of the classroom is a systematic, data-oriented approach. It manages pupils and relies on positive reinforcement as a major way of maximizing their performance. It specifies the behaviors and the consequences for those behaviors. It is data-oriented in that it captures and reports the data associated with those behaviors and uses those data to evaluate the effectiveness of the management procedure. If there is no data, there is no behavior modification program.

Behavior modification, after a long and arduous struggle to gain a foothold in psychological and educational settings, has suddenly become highly used. Unfortunately, it now has an acceptance that borders on pop psychology. Many practitioners have insufficient understanding of the principles and practices of the discipline but use it as if they were experts. Like any powerful tool, it can be misunderstood and misused by practitioners with inadequate training or supervision. The result is that the entire school of thought gets a black eye and its use is rejected, when, in fact, its misuse is responsible. Ask for the data.

Classroom Management

A fundamental rule about teaching is that the teacher is able to control the students and the classroom environment. It doesn't much matter whether this means one student or a group of thirty to forty. To the degree that the teacher is not able to control the behavior of the students, chaos is introduced. To the extent that chaos exists, instruction suffers. This control is not dictatorial, based on fear and loathing, but on a relationship between the teacher and the student(s) in which each recognizes and accepts a particular role for the mutual benefit of everyone else.

For the teacher, this fundamental rule boils down to "I say. You do." The relationship between any teacher and student is predicated on the assumption that the teacher is the repository of information, knowledge and/or skills which the student needs but does not yet have. The teacher's role is to impart as efficiently and thoroughly as possible that information, knowledge or skills to the learner.

The Learner's Role

The learner's fundamental task is to acquire this information or knowledge of skills as quickly and completely as possible. That necessitates the students placing themselves under the instructional control of the teacher. Acknowledgment of the teacher's control is manifested in listening carefully, following instructions, being coached, watching demonstrations, taking corrections, making new attempts and paying attention to warnings, encouragement and other feedback the teacher provides.

The situation also assumes that the teacher has something important to teach, has the ability to instruct and the skills to manage the student or class.

Many people, including some educators who currently train teachers, believe that teachers are born, not made. Behaviorists believe the opposite, that like other skills, teaching skills can and must be learned.

In most teacher-training programs, classroom management is given short shrift. It is often erroneously equated with discipline and left in the hands of the principal or vice-principal. "Discipline", as it is traditionally viewed, is out of favor in today's schools. While there is reason to celebrate the banning of corporal punishment in schools, there is also the need to provide teachers and principals with effective classroom management skills and a range of options to teach children self-management as well as social and personal responsibility.

The Current Craze - Child-Centered Learning

The "child-centered" approach to teaching is among the recent bandwagons whose effects permeate the modern classroom. Loosely based on developmental theories like Piaget's, which describe development as a series of ages and stages, these misapplied principles wind up being translated into "readiness to learn" practices which place control of the curriculum largely in the hands of the learner. This leads to a reliance on the child eventually discovering the way things work through trial and error manipulation of the environment.

The End Result of "Discovery Learning"

The modern child, when asked what he learned today, replies, "Nothing, but I gained some meaningful insights." - Bill Vaughan

Unfortunately, in all too many instances, the children never "discover" how to read, spell, write or do arithmetic. The usual defense for this lack of progress is that the child has not yet progressed to the appropriate stage in order to be able to discover how to do this particular activity. The child is not "ready". One question these advocates have never answered to my satisfaction is, "If these students are not 'ready' to learn to read, what skills are they 'ready' to learn that will get them 'ready to learn' to read?" If we can compile a laundry list of these skills, we, as teachers, have something to do. If these pre-skills to academic activities like learning to read cannot be specified, or if they can be specified but not influenced by instruction, we may rightly ask, "What is the teacher's role in learning?"

Some Basics of Classroom Management

Above all, the teacher's role is to manage the students and their behavior in the classroom setting. This is generally most easily done by developing a short set of rules, teaching them to the students and applying them consistently.

In our school, there were five basic rules:

1. Work quickly and quietly.
2. Bring all of your materials to class.
3. Keep your hands and feet to yourself.
4. Say only good things.
5. Raise your hand to address the class.

Each of these rules specify behaviors that can be easily observed and have ready consequences. They are positively stated so that the student knows what to do and what not to do. They are binary in that they can be answered by a simple "yes" or "no". The student is either working quickly or quietly or he is not. He either has all of the necessary materials or not. There are far fewer judgment calls and more consistency and fairness. Also these rules are general enough to cover most situations.

Consistency in rewarding compliance and in withholding reward for infringements become the critical determinants in evaluating the effectiveness of the process.

The most efficient method of managing classroom or learner behavior is to teach well. Students who are involved are not behavior problems. If the instruction is too fast, too slow, too easy or too difficult, students may become behavior problems.

Attention as a Reinforcer

Humans are gregarious by nature. They tend to organize themselves into families, groups and communities. They display high levels of social and personal interaction in most cases. Historically, one of the most excessive punishments for misbehavior is to be ostracized. Even withholding attention can be punishing for many humans.

Teacher Attention

It becomes important to know how powerful attention is to students. Like all humans, students seek attention more frequently from some people than others. Students also seek attention more in some situations than in others. Teacher attention, especially during instructional periods, can be a major source of reward for most students. Major determinant behaviors to which the teacher incidentally or purposely attends' are likely to be strengthened as a direct result of having been rewarded with attention.

The Criticism Trap

Perhaps the use of attention to foster appropriate behavior is best described by using a non-example of good classroom management commonly known as the criticism trap.

Imagine a classroom where one student, Jimmy, is frequently getting out of his seat for any number of reasons. He often sharpens his pencil, makes frequent trips to the wastebasket, visits the bookshelves and other areas of the classroom to get or return things. He is out of his seat several times a period.

Each time Jimmy leaves his seat, his teacher asks him to sit down. He explains that he needs to sharpen his pencil or whatever, does so and returns to his desk. Although this may not constitute a serious behavior problem, it is hardly the thing any teacher wants in his classroom. (Imagine if all the students began doing this!) It is probably having some effect on Jimmy's work production. It's a poor model for other students and could be disruptive to effective teaching.

At first glance, this may not look like a trap. When Jimmy is admonished for leaving his seat, he returns to it. The teacher feels that the behavior is under control. If, however, you charted Jimmy's out-of-seat behavior over time, you would most likely find that it is not changed by the teacher's criticism. It occurs with a consistent frequency across days and weeks.

The Trap

The trap lies in the fact that the teacher is being rewarded for being critical. Each time he tells Jimmy to sit down, he does so. But the overall frequency of out-of-seat behavior is not decreasing. In fact, the teacher may be strengthening or maintaining the very behavior he wishes to eliminate by paying attention to it.

The trap also lies in the fact that Jimmy may be being systematically paid off with attention for doing exactly what the teacher doesn't want. He may seek attention, not by participating in the class, but by leaving his seat.

To test the attention as a trap hypothesis, the teacher should reward Jimmy with attention for being on task in his seat and systematically never reward his out-of-seat behavior. He might even reward the children around him for appropriate "in-seat" behavior as a way of showing him what behaviors will and will not be rewarded. If attention is a reinforcer for Jimmy, the frequency of his out-of-seat behavior should change. It should decrease over days until it approximates the frequency of the rest of the class.

Sometimes teacher attention is not a reinforcer of student behavior and will not immediately accomplish the task of getting a student to be more compliant. At that point other options exist.

When Attention is not Enough - A Case Study - "Madame" and her Francs

Lynne Brearley is a superb French teacher in an elementary school in Belleville, Ontario. To her adoring eight to twelve-year-old students, she is simply known as "Madame".

Sixteen years ago, however, when she began her career as a second language teacher, things were somewhat different. She was faced with several huge classes of hormonal Grade 7 and 8 students who made it quite clear to her from the outset that French was just not cool. They hated it and had no intention of learning to like it. A few of the more boisterous adolescents took a certain pride in being inattentive and uncooperative, and in some ways they set the tone for the rest of the class.

During September, Madame forged ahead with the curriculum but her lessons were often interrupted by inappropriate behavior, warnings, frequent detentions and visits to the principal. By the end of the month, she was stressed out and frustrated, for she knew that if she could just get control of the whole group, she could deliver a quality program.

I suggested some behavior modification approaches, and with the help of her sister, Judie, a local high school vice-principal, their artistic juices began flowing. They designed a management program which she still uses to this day.

With green paper, Madame created "Francs" with an attractive fleur-de-lis symbol, a school bank name and lines for the date and the student's name. Armed with a pocketful of these on Monday morning, she began putting them on the desks of students who were sitting quietly in their seats. The curiosity of almost everyone was immediately piqued. More were awarded for raising hands, answering questions or giving it their best shot, even if the answer wasn't linguistically perfect. By the end of the period, almost everyone had a Franc, for by complimenting the behavior she was looking for each time, it became obvious what one had to do to earn one of these strange green slips of paper.

Madame had the students sign their Francs and explained that at the end of the month there would be a special draw, but only those with Francs would be allowed to participate.

Competition to earn one each class became fierce. Every day the students worked harder and acted more appropriately. Madame was careful never to give a Franc to a student who didn't raise his hand but merely blurted out the answer. Students who were slouched in their seats never got one until they sat straighter. If good behavior was followed by bad, Madame simply took the student's Franc and put it back in her pocket.

Participation, academic performance, following classroom rules, cooperation and kindness to others were all rewarded. Anyone could earn a Franc. All you had to do was try.

The first month's "tirage" (draw) was a big hit, even if the six prizes weren't particularly expensive. Special pencils, a chocolate bar or two, a small game - all were won with clapping, congratulations and excitement at the chance of having one's Franc pulled out from the pile in the box.

Within the month, even the behavior of the most recalcitrant students had changed dramatically. They would be sitting quietly when Madame arrived at the door; they would pay attention and try hard to participate. They sang the French songs a little louder and played the games with more enthusiasm.

All this effort, of course, resulted in new verbal and written French skills. French became not only cool, but fun! The students were enthusiastic and proud of their accomplishments. Madame was ecstatic. She had arrived.

Over the years, since that first rambunctious group of students, Lynne has refined the system and has expanded its use to each of her French classes. The younger children can hardly wait to get to Grade 3 so they can start learning French with Madame. Former students who have finished University still meet her on the street and fondly remember her Francs and the monthly draws. With a little imagination and some simple but solid behavior modification, Lynne Brearley turned her job from potential burnout to pure pleasure, while engendering a love of French in thousands of young, competent students.

Behavior Management of Adult Students

Adult students who are not keen to learn are often more subtle in their approach. They are long past the juvenile outbursts that younger students may try. Some adult students simply attempt to direct the teacher's attention away from instruction by inviting conversation. They ask an unrelated question, attempt to involve the teacher in a discussion of their personal concerns and/or complaints. They sometimes use up a lot of instructional time with understanding teachers in discussions totally unrelated to the academic topic at hand. This is another form of attention as a trap. For the teacher, it is often easier to discuss something with a student than it is to teach a boring or difficult piece of curriculum. The teacher is rewarded because he doesn't have to work as diligently and he may be genuinely interested in the student's issue, even to the point of feeling that he should be involved or at least attentive and sympathetic. The student is reinforced for talking about problems or concerns and systematically not rewarded for performing academic work. It may also result in less independent work or less homework being able to be assigned because the instruction was not completed in class. The student's progress slows down and allows him to fall behind in his program, and possibly fail.

Performance Contracts

With adults, we tend not to use the same type of reward

structure that we would employ with children. The use of tokens would probably be viewed as demeaning by most grown-ups. Instead, a contract of rights and responsibilities is negotiated with each individual. This contract specifies the requirements for attendance, punctuality, work completion and general deportment while at the center. It also details the center's responsibility to the student.

Attendance

In many instances, adult clients who come to Quinte Learning Center have been enrolled in other programs where the expectations were not explicit or were not enforced. Attendance was either not taken or not reported back to agencies, so that caseworkers never knew if a student was doing well or poorly or even going to class. Sometimes clients could be enrolled in a program for months, making little or no progress, becoming hopelessly lost, and their caseworker would never know that they had finally dropped or failed out of the program.

This situation makes for serious problems for caseworkers and clients. It is wasteful both in terms of time, money and effort for all concerned. To avoid this situation, our contracts specify the terms of attendance with the specific dates being detailed. This allows the caseworker to track student performance in terms of attendance. It also makes it easy to spot students who could become problematic, often the ones who tend to be absent on Fridays or Mondays.

Academic Production

The contract also specifies the amount of work to be successfully completed by the student during each day. If a student is enrolled in the literacy program, he is expected to finish a total of 15 lessons daily from various parts of the curriculum.

In the upgrading program, the teacher determines the homework assignments with an understanding of how long each student is expected to be at the center before entering a post-secondary academic course of study, training or job search.

In the initial intake interview, a plan of academic needs and the estimated time to meet them is developed. This is sent to the caseworker in a written report which sets the benchmarks for academic production during enrollment at Quinte Learning Center. Monthly reports outline academic progress with this initial plan as a frame of reference. Decisions concerning continuing in the program can be based on these data. If the center has failed to get the student to the objective in the time specified, despite the student's continued best efforts, the center teaches that student for free until the objectives have been met.

Punctuality

Adult students are expected to treat their courses as a work program. That assumes that the student will be on time. If this begins to become problematic, it is also noted in the monthly report.

Daily Reporting

Each day, teachers report on the progress of each of their students regarding punctuality, attendance, homework completion and lessons covered that day. Other comments are noted for the manager's attention. These reports are kept in a day book which the manager reviews daily. The information allows the manager to reward students for their good work and to discern problems as they emerge. If a problem is of a more urgent nature, it might be reported to the manager immediately by the teacher, rather than simply written as a part of the day-book report.

In this way, problems can be attended to quickly. Congratulations and kudos can be given easily while the accomplishment is still fresh in the student's mind. The day book becomes a source from which the monthly report is generated.

Monthly Reporting

The monthly report gives the student, the caseworker, the teacher and the manager sufficient information to determine how well a student is progressing. It allows problems to be communicated early in the student's program if they exist. It allows for monthly recommendations to the caseworker if the student is not able or willing to honor the contract. It is the basis for discussion and decisions regarding each student and his tenure with us.

Summary

In order to establish control in the teaching environment, behavior management strategies are used. They vary widely depending on the characteristics of the students and their particular needs. The use of this technology ensures that the students know what is expected of them, what they can expect from the setting and what the consequences are for all parties in any set of circumstances.

Teaching teachers and managers to become skillful behavior analysts and practitioners does take some time and energy, but it is not rocket science. It is often more difficult to teach them to vary the content of their feedback to students (verbal reinforcers) so that they do not always say the same thing, than it is to teach them the fundamental principles and practices of behavior analysis.

Now that the student is under the instructional control of the teacher, the actual teaching can begin. The process of successfully teaching basic literacy and numeracy skills is addressed in the following chapter in our discussion of Direct Instruction.

Direct Instruction

· ·

"If a child can get from the door to the chair
without feeling the walls, you can teach him to read."
- Zig Engelmann

What is it?

Direct Instruction is first and foremost an instructional design technology. It is a method of presenting information so that it is easily learned by every student. Direct Instruction has numerous rules and conventions. It relies on applied research and extensive field trials to develop a series of instructional sequences into an educational program that will most effectively teach a portion of the school's basic curriculum such as reading, math, or spelling to any and all students.

Perhaps the best short description of Direct Instruction and its research is a chapter by Becker and Carnine in *Advances in Clinical Child Psychology, Vol. 3.* (1980). A more in-depth presentation can be found in *Theory of Instruction* (1982) by Engelmann and Carnine. *Preventing Failure in the Primary Grades* (1969) or *War Against The Schools' Academic Child Abuse* (1992) by Engelmann make good reading in plain English.

Where did it come from?

It's obvious from the publication dates of the books cited above and from the dates defining the era of Project Follow Through that Direct Instruction has been around for a number of years. Direct Instruction was originally created by Zig Engelmann and his colleagues including Elaine Bruner, Jean Osborne and Carl Bereiter at the University of Illinois in the 1960s. It began as a series of programs for culturally disadvantaged children in a preschool at the University of Illinois at Urbana-Champaign.

In 1973, Wes Becker convinced Engelmann to relocate to the University of Oregon and become a member of its faculty. They were soon joined by Doug Carnine, who quickly became Engelmann's close associate, co-author and research partner. Direct Instruction became the preferred educational technology of the Department of Special Education at the University of Oregon. It was expanded into a set of programs that became the dominant model in the Follow Through project in the seventies.

Zig Engelmann has a bachelor's degree. He never got a Ph.D., nor has he ever attempted to do so; yet he is a full professor at the University of Oregon who continually refuses tenure.

It seems that Engelmann was working for a marketing company in Illinois, doing a project to promote some publisher's reading materials. When he visited a classroom and saw how poorly the materials taught the children, he decided to write a reading program himself. He literally sat down and wrote his first teaching sequences, outlined a program and took it to Carl Bereiter at the University of Illinois.

The Distar Series

When the first cohort of students began the Follow Through project, Engelmann and his colleagues created a group of ten programs for use in their sites. Each of three programs taught reading, language skills and arithmetic. One small program, attached to the second reading program, taught spelling. Distar is an acronym which stands for Direct Instruction System for Teaching And Remediation.

Each of the nine larger programs in the Distar series contained 180 lessons, one lesson for each school day. The students would be enrolled in all three programs and would complete one level of programming in each subject area in each of the three years of the Follow Through project.

Engelmann and his co-workers lived with the rational hope that if they could prove the superiority of their programs, teachers and administrators would adopt them for their and their students' benefit. The results did, in fact, support the thesis that Direct Instruction accomplished better results than any other model in the Follow Through study. Despite the fact that these programs were published by a leading educational publisher, Science Research Associates, and marketed internationally, the wholesale acceptance Engelmann had hoped for did not occur.

Learning Disability Legislation

In the early eighties, the U.S. Congress passed Bill 42-192, which enshrined the rights of students with learning difficulties, providing them special education assistance by law. Similar legislation, Bill 82, was passed in the Ontario legislature the following year. Most provinces and states have some form of special education bill dating from this period. These laws stipulated that all students with a "learning disability" would be provided special assistance to remediate their condition so that they would be successful at school. Each student would undergo academic and, in some cases, other testing. They would be diagnosed, and then be given an individualized program plan followed by appropriate remediation. The plan was to outline the remediation, track the progress and report to the appropriate authorities and to the parents.

The Corrective Series

Frustrated by the lack of acceptance of his Distar programs, Engelmann took a new tack. He assumed that teachers would be looking for effective teaching strategies for these learning disabled students. He and the group in Oregon created a number of remedial-education programs in reading, reading comprehension, arithmetic, spelling and writing, thinking that if the law insisted on adequate remediation, schools would select the best available instructional programs for this new initiative.

As with the Distar programs, the Corrective series was designed to provide a full year's curriculum at each level in all the basic subjects. They were completely field tested and had applied research to support their effectiveness. Again, although the programs were successful, they did not enjoy success in relation to the size of the problem or the needs of the children.

The Mastery Series

As the educational pendulum swung back to a basal series of texts for each classroom in the middle 1980s, Engelmann and his co-authors created yet another set of Direct Instruction programs in core curriculum areas for elementary instruction.

This series of programs was adopted by some schools, but was actively resisted by some districts. In fact, when it was rejected by the California Textbook Adoption Committee, Engelmann successfully sued the State of California to force its inclusion on the list of texts approved for use in California schools.

As with the previous series, each Mastery Reading program contains sufficient curriculum to cover a year's work at each level. Each of the programs is field tested and each is revised periodically as new research indicates areas of strength and weakness.

How Does it Work?

Direct Instruction programs work in a particular way. There are specific materials, specific activities for both the teacher and student and specific procedures to be followed within the daily lesson.

Each program is part of an integrated series that is meant

to be used at the grade level where that curriculum would usually be taught. The programs are sequenced such that there is
a level for each grade until that curriculum has been completely covered. Ensuring that the curriculum has been covered is done by providing a scope and sequence chart of the
skills taught in each program in the series. This chart outlines
in detail what is included in the program and the order in
which it will be taught, reviewed and tested.

The Series Guide

A Series Guide is provided to outline all of the concepts
and operations in each level of the program. The guide also
provides the placement tests, a description of the series, sample formats, and extensive instructions for the teacher. This
approach ensures that each teacher is aware of all of the segments of the series, what will have been taught by previous
teachers, what he is to teach and what will be added to the
program by teachers in the following grades.

Teacher and Student Materials

Each program contains a Teacher's Presentation book.
These are significantly different than other published programs in that each book contains scripted formats for each
activity in each lesson. This is not some general set of hints as
to how the teacher might proceed. It is a complete set of
instructions that tells the teacher what to say and what to
expect the students to say in response. The Direct Instruction
teacher does not go home at night and try to dream up some
strategy to teach some child or group of children a particular
skill or set of skills the next day. The lessons are completely
provided so that the teacher needs only to follow the script.
The objectives will be covered by the end of the program.

The difference is similar to that between a Shakespearean
play and improv. theater. No Shakespearean actor would come
on stage and wing the soliloquy to Yorick by Hamlet. He
would recite the soliloquy the way the Bard wrote it, word for

word. His delivery might differ in a dozen different ways, being highly individual, but the words would remain the same. Many teachers, whether they wish to or not, are forced to perform the equivalent of improv. everyday because their programs do not provide any script to assist them.

Each lesson is divided into several tasks to vary the lesson, provide new material and review previously taught skills. Many of the Direct Instruction scripts also include specific correction procedures to assist the teacher in dealing with incorrect answers. Each Teacher's Presentation Manual contains a list of the behavioral objectives the program is intended to cover, recording forms and answer keys for all assigned written tasks. It also includes test materials, remedial activities and class charts to record points earned by the groups in the class.

The student materials are usually consumable workbooks with lessons to accompany each of those in the teacher's materials. In some programs, such as the Mastery Reading Series, there are also non-consumable texts.

Activities

Placement Tests

Every program contains a placement test which is intended to be administered to each student at the beginning of the school year. The placement test will assist the teacher in placing the students at the appropriate program level. Sometimes teachers schedule their reading periods simultaneously and will stream two or more classes of students into reading groups to achieve greater homogeneity in each reading group.

Grouping the Students

Typically the class is divided into several groups depending on their performance on the placement test for the program. A typical class of thirty regular elementary students would be divided into two or three groups. The largest group would consist of the most easily taught students who already have a significant skill set as indicated by their scores on the placement test. This group might have fifteen or more students. The second group of students would be smaller and would be made up of those who placed in the program according to the placement test, but who have lower test scores and may need more instruction and more corrections than the first larger group. The final group consists of the four or five lowest performing children in the class. They will require the greatest amount of teacher time and instruction.

The groups are not set in stone. Children may move from one group to another depending on performance.

Scheduling Instruction

Having grouped the children, the teacher's objective is to cover one lesson with each group, every day, for all of the programs he has set up in the class. To do so, the teacher would typically provide a 40 to 45-minute reading and math instruction period during each day. Starting with the smallest group, he would then repeat the lesson with the second smaller group and finally with the third largest and highest performing group. As each group finishes its instruction, the members would use the rest of the period to complete the assignments in their workbooks. Having been taught first, those in the lowest performing group have more time to complete their assignment. They can listen in twice more to the instruction if necessary as it is presented to the others to reinforce the skills taught and review the seatwork. The largest group can work independently on the seatwork assignment, doing those review exercises which have been covered in previous lessons. Children who miss time, or who still need more repetition can be paired with the top students for peer tutoring and can do the same lesson again later that day if necessary.

Ensuring Success

The Direct Instruction programs are designed to teach

every child all of the skills in the program. This is achieved by placing the students in groups of relatively similar performance levels and by teaching each group to a high criterion of correct answers. All errors are corrected. Corrective feedback is immediate, non-critical, and specific to the error. The error is corrected as a group so no child is ever singled out for making a mistake. Such repetition is not wasted on the other students.

Each lesson is divided into formats, some of which introduce material to teach new skills, some of which review and reinforce previously taught skills with a range of new examples of the concept or operation. The students know that the skill presented in the lesson will be used immediately in the independent work and will be part of their lessons from this point on. They get a wealth of opportunity to apply the skills immediately and often in successive lessons. The format remains part of the program in future lessons so that the student is provided intermittent practice and testing on any skill developed by the program.

Teacher Behavior

Perhaps the most dramatic visual difference between Direct Instruction and other programs is to be seen in the teacher's behavior. Direct Instruction is based on the premise that quality teacher instruction is a critical variable in student success. Delivery should be as fast paced as reasonably possible. The teaching should proceed quickly enough to force the students' attention to the lesson without pushing them into unnecessary errors. Children who are attentive and active in learning tend not to be behavior problems. The very best way to solve inappropriate behavior in a classroom is to have the students engaged in lessons which will provide them with success on meaningful skills. Direct Instruction does this better than any other teaching technology.

The added benefit of teaching faster is that there is more opportunity for the students to respond, to firm up the learning so that they can work independently, and to correct errors and strengthen newly learned skills.

"Children have more need of models than of critics." - Joubert

Teaching Direct Instruction typically means that the teacher will follow a procedure called "Model - Lead - Test". He will originally model the task for the students so that they can understand what the correct answer is and, equally important, what it is not, as well as the steps to getting to the correct answer. After modeling the task, the students will repeat the procedure with the teacher. This is known as "the lead". Finally, when the teacher has led the students through the process until he is content that they know it, he gives them a chance to do it independently, thereby testing their ability to do the task. Once the students can perform quickly and accurately, individual turns are given to check on anyone of concern before taking the group through the related examples on their worksheets and assigning their seatwork.

Correcting Errors

Although Direct Instruction teachers work at a faster than normal pace, they also monitor the instruction continuously for errors. One critical dimension of quality Direct Instruction is in its attention to correcting errors. The fundamental rule is that every error is corrected as soon as it is made. This ensures that every student in the group can do each format correctly before the teacher moves on to the next segment. It also makes sure that every student is learning, that each individual can respond accurately to the oral segment of the lesson and do the assigned seatwork with an acceptable level of errors. Getting rid of these errors when they occur prevents students from becoming progressively more confused and lost in the instruction, accompanied by all of the detrimental effects associated with not knowing how to do something. If some students are having a lot of difficulty with a particular format, the teacher may alternate that format so that he presents it, then does a second task. The teacher then returns to the difficult format and continues to alternate it with others so that the students get the additional instructions and corrections in measured doses rather than being bogged down on some part of the lesson, becoming frustrated or discouraged. Bonus points would typically be given for mastering the format.

Feedback, Praise and Rewards

Another teacher behavior that is generally more frequent in a Direct Instruction program is in the level of feedback and encouragement of the students' efforts. Praise is specifically written into the scripted lessons to prompt the teacher to reward good performances by the students.

The well-trained D.I. teacher continuously encourages his students. Comments like, "This is hard, but I know how smart you are." or " We can do this one!" or "That's close, let's do that one more time." are made to urge students to give their best efforts.

"You got it!", "That's bang on!", "Nice going, you're right!" are frequently used by competent D.I. instructors. It's important to vary the wording of the verbal reward statements so that they don't become banal and pedestrian. Usually the teacher is excited about the students doing good work and that excitement comes through naturally in the feedback.

Learning as a Reward

Many times, praise and feedback are not the only reinforcers which encourage performance. Often learning a task is its own reward. Tom, a man in his mid-forties, is a perfect example of this. Having worked as a farmer and a back-hoe operator since the age of 12, Tom was injured and came to the Quinte Learning Center for retraining. He had a warm and friendly smile, a soft voice, a gentle manner, and he couldn't read a single word.

After an academic assessment, Tom was placed in the most basic level of the reading program which teaches the sounds that letters make. He worked hard and progressed quickly. He had three teenage children at home who enjoyed helping their Dad with his homework.

At the end of his six-month tenure at QLC, Tom was able to read Grade 7 level material in addition to completing Grade 5 level spelling and Grade 8 mathematics. Everyone was pleased with the tremendous progress he had made and expressions of congratulations were in abundance.

Nothing pleased him more, however, than when, on his 20th wedding anniversary a month previous, he had gone into a shop, for the first time ever, to pick out a card for his wife. He meticulously read through all of them, chose his favorite, and signed it with his name and an "I love you". For most of us, a task such as this approaches the mundane. For Tom, it was one of pride and pure joy.

The Emotional Payoffs

Perhaps the most strikingly obvious difference in the behavior of a D.I. teacher is the enthusiasm with which instruction is delivered. The smooth teaching of concepts and operations is stimulating for both teacher and students. It lends excitement to the process. The constant flow of correct answers builds confidence in the learners. The feeling of control they gain by knowing their teacher will work with them until they can do it right allows children to take chances. The knowledge that any error will be corrected without criticism and without making them feel badly is reassuring, especially to those students who perceive themselves as not as competent as their peers. The constant corrective feedback that gets them back on track is a safety net. The encouragement that they can do it and that "if they work hard, they will get smart" makes being in the class fun. It builds further confidence, knowing that they are capable of great learning. Also being held accountable to work hard, to complete their assignments and to help the class learn is a good lesson in and of itself.

The fact that the Direct Instruction model in Project Follow Through received the highest scores on the affective tests is a reflection of the degree to which these teacher behaviors positively affect children, influencing their self-perception and how they feel about their learning.

Seatwork Assignments and Tests

Once the teacher assigns the seatwork for one group, the next group begins its instruction. The seatwork provided by the programs alleviates the need for the teacher to be continually designing and providing exercises for the class. This frees up valuable time for marking, individual attention to students, charting progress and program evaluation.

The seatwork assignments and in-program tests also provide a continuous flow of information regarding student progress, allowing the teacher to make decisions about review or in some instances even skipping formats.

Other Teacher Behaviors

The D.I. teacher aims his instructional presentation to the lowest-performing member of the group with the idea that when this student can handle the task, the group can safely move on. The teacher is governed by the basic rule that if the student didn't learn, the teacher didn't teach. For 25 years these programs have shown their capacity to get the job done, so teachers can generally infer that if there is a problem, it is more likely to be in the delivery of the instruction than in its design. A review of their own performance will most likely provide insights into what needs to be changed.

Like all teachers, D.I. instructors make mistakes. The difference between a competent D.I. teacher and some others in the profession is that the former learns not to be afraid to look bad in front of the students. In fact, the teacher making errors imparts a valuable lesson about how to handle making a mistake. Generally the teacher just admits it and does the task again, hopefully correctly. The students love it when they catch a teacher out. It can actually heighten attention and facilitate the lesson. When all of the students are editing the teacher's behavior for a mistake, they are also paying strict attention to the presentation and are more likely to learn.

If, on the other hand, a student makes an error and is subjected to any criticism by another student, the teacher will intervene to preserve the child's self-esteem. The rule about "Say only good things" is immediately invoked. Any repetition usually results in a loss of points for that student. The teacher does acknowledge that the answer is incorrect, but doesn't personalize the error. He treats it as an opportunity to redo the task, so that the student does it correctly. He may also monitor that student's responses more carefully, giving him more frequent individual turns to make sure he has learned the skill.

Direct Instruction teachers also remind students of their past learning to show them that they are capable of performing well. They have a history of doing so and, based on that, they should feel confident of what they are going to learn next. "We did one of these in the last lesson. You can do it!" is typical of this kind of encouragement.

Why Does It Work?

The high frequency of student response, the correction of each and every error and the continual praise and encouragement might lead observers to conclude that these are the features that make Direct Instruction work. They would be only partly right. These are attributes which assist in the smooth, reliable delivery of a Direct Instruction curriculum. They are important, but the essence of Direct Instruction is not as much in its delivery, as it is in its design.

Direct Instruction presents concepts and operations so that they have one and only one possible interpretation. That way the teacher is sure of the interpretation the student has learned from the lesson. To the extent that any presentation allows for more than one possible meaning, the students may adopt some interpretation not intended by the teacher as being the correct one. The teacher only discerns this when feedback from the student indicates that the student has understood the lesson differently than planned. While this may be permissible and even encouraged in the study of poetry or abstract art, it is less than helpful when teaching a child to decode words or to do math or science problems. One way to ensure the correct interpretation is to teach the learner rules that can be reliably applied.

Making Rules Explicit

Whenever a rule can be derived that covers an entire set of examples reliably, it is stated explicitly and taught to the student. For example, in teaching fractions, the teacher will teach the student the rule about the denominator (bottom part) of the fraction: "The bottom part of a fraction tells you how many parts are in each group." This rule works for the bottom parts of all fractions, but it is rarely made clear in math texts or teacher demonstrations. The failure to make this rule explicit sometimes makes fractions more difficult to understand. There are many, many rules that can be extracted from the elementary school curriculum. Most of us have learned a few, for example, "i" before "e" except after "c"; change the "y" to "i" and add "es" to make a "y" ending plural. These rules are helpful and we even remember them many years later. In current public education such rules are rarely taught.

One of the Direct Instruction remedial spelling programs, Corrective Spelling through Morphographs, contains fourteen clear-cut spelling rules. When applied to the possible combinations of 640 morphographs (word parts), this allows the learner to spell more than 12,000 words. This program has 140 lessons and can easily be covered in a school year.

If one follows the more traditional method of the 25-word weekly spelling list with a test on Friday, and does so religiously from Grade 2 through Grade 8, a student would learn 1,000 words per year or a total of 7,000 words during his entire elementary school career.

Teachers, however, have rarely been trained to this level of instructional design. And after a hard day of teaching, it is a little much to ask the teacher to go home and crank out several instructionally sound lessons in various areas of curriculum for the next day. Writing these formats into lessons and finally as programs requires a great deal of time, effort and skill. With Direct Instruction programs, that becomes unnecessary. The program has already been masterfully designed and written. The teacher can concentrate on delivering solid curriculum with the knowledge that all of these design aspects have been considered, included and field tested before the program was sold to the school.

Summary

Direct Instruction represents the current pinnacle of instructional design technology. It has a long and impressive empirical history in a wide number of settings with a host of various clients. It works better than other instructional efforts because it is a total entity, taking into account the curriculum design requirements and the instructional delivery components. It covers the motivational aspects of the students' behavior and consistently provides encouragement and rewards for improved performance. It is geared to teach every child in the class and assumes that producing learning is the responsibility of the teacher.

Direct Instruction programs teach the general case. In learning to teach one Direct Instruction program, the teacher is, in fact, learning about teaching all of the D.I. programs. Most of the same behaviors that are required to teach one program are used consistently in every other. Although the content changes, the formats are done in the same way, making it easy to adapt from one to another.

Caution

The term "direct instruction" is becoming popular in current teacher jargon. One must be very sure that the person is talking about the same Direct Instruction discussed here. There is no generic model of Direct Instruction.

Precision Teaching

● ●

"What gets measured, gets done."
- Drucker

What is it?

Precision Teaching is a measurement and decision-making technology which uses frequency and rate of change in the behavior as its basic data. The frequency of the response is measured one or more times as needed on a daily basis. When frequency is counted over time, it is the classical scientific measure for rate (e.g. miles per hour, sales per day, words per minute). Rate and rate of change of the performance become the basic data for the student.

The same kind of measure is common with economic and other scientific indices. In business, the equity markets track thousands of stocks, each with various prices and rates of change. They deal with different exchanges in diverse currencies minute by minute. The results are presented graphically and are easily interpreted by millions of people looking at a myriad of shares on global exchanges. In science, the rate of speed of the Jupiter probe tells NASA when it will reach various destinations. The same kind of rate measurement, known as Precision Teaching, has been applied to education.

Where did it come from?

Precision Teaching was pioneered by Ogden R. Lindsley,

while he was a doctoral student of B.F. Skinner. Skinner founded the study of operant conditioning, behavior analysis and behavior modification at Harvard University in the 1950s.

Precision Teaching grew out of the laboratory research being done by Lindsley at Harvard. He noted that the records kept on the Skinner boxes (where pigeons pecked at keys to obtain food, or rats pressed on a bar to receive food pellets) were capturing the rate of response of these animals. These records were kept by cumulative recorders, a wheel with a paper roll that turned at a constant speed. Each time the subject responded, a pen would mark the paper on the recorder. Skinner and Charles Ferster had determined that different schedules of delivering the food led to different patterns of responses by the animals as they learned to be highly efficient in pecking or pressing for food.

As the rate of response increased or decreased, the slope of the line on the paper would rise or fall concurrently. If the animal was given food after each response, a stable low intensity of pecks occurred. If the food was made available at five-minute intervals, the pigeon or the rat learned to wait until the time was almost up and then respond rapidly in a short burst. (A little like students writing term papers or people doing Christmas shopping.) Different schedules of reward produced different patterns of response.

Lindsley became fascinated by the concept of frequency of response and by the idea of looking at response rates over time to see the changes in the behavior. Postulating that there might be similar learning rates in man, he became interested in applying the same types of measures to human behavior. Is the rate of response (i.e. words read in a period of time) for "good" readers different than for "poor" ones? Are "slow" students really slow?

Kids and Charts

Lindsley designed a version of the laboratory cumulative recorder on paper which he called the Standard Behavior Chart. Like the cumulative recorder, it measures the frequency and rate of change of behaviors.

He then accepted a position at the University of Kansas, with the intention of using this new measurement technology to investigate the academic performances of children in basic curriculum. He soon found out that students' behavior did vary over time. The data did reflect the learning of the children. Poor readers did read more slowly and with more errors than good readers. "Slow" students have slower rates of response, with a higher frequency of errors. As Lindsley worked with the students, he refined the Standard Behavior Chart and began developing a methodology for its use in schools. Eric Haughton, who later taught me this technology, was one of Lindsley's first two doctoral students and played a significant role in the development of this new measurement technology.

The Standard Celeration Chart

The chart allows the teacher, the student or both to select a behavior and measure its frequency each day for a period as long as twenty weeks, monitoring the rate of increase or decrease of the behavior.

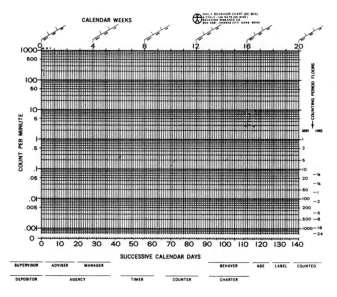

121

What this means is that an entire school year of a student's performance in one subject area can be captured on two sheets of paper. The chart becomes an historical record of the student's behavior. It changes qualitatively and quantitatively. Program changes, other strategies, teacher interventions and associated problems can all be noted over the 40 weeks of school.

There are also Standard Celeration Charts for weekly, monthly, annual and decade measures. Data can be summarized across these time periods to allow direct comparison of results of individuals or groups.

Why Measure Frequency?

Frequency is a universal measure. Every behavior has a frequency or a range of frequencies, from the rate of occurrence of continental glaciers every ten thousand or so years to the beat of a hummingbird's wings at about one thousand per minute. But despite its universal presence, frequency is not a measure humans often pay much attention to. Many of us might know our resting heart rate. Some people have a general idea of their respiration rate. Very few people, however, know the rate at which they walk or the range of rates at which they read, speak or do many of the things they do daily, and have been doing for years. They simply don't think of their own behavior in those terms, and are even somewhat surprised when someone else does. How fast do you talk? Why would anyone want to know? If I am helping in the speech rehabilitation of a stroke victim, it would be beneficial to know the rate at which normal conversation occurs as part of my treatment measure.

If you go into an emergency room, frequency becomes much more carefully and frequently monitored. ER technicians want to know the frequency of many things accurately and often. The more critical the situation, the more they demand such data. Not bad for a science that only a couple of centuries ago measured nothing.

Educators have not followed suit. In fact, as learning prob-

122

lems occur in unsuccessful students, the process is much more likely to be slowed down, reduced in intensity and measured less, rather than more frequently.

In education, as in other "helping" professions, there need to be better methods of documentation of the efforts of its practitioners and the impact of those efforts on the learner. How does the teacher know that his teaching is successful unless they can measure its effects within some reasonable period?

Frequencies are Observable and Repeatable

If we know how well we read aloud, we could easily determine whether our ability falls within the accepted range of competent oral readers. The range is considered to be 200 to 250 words per minute with two or fewer errors. Most people are surprised that it is that high and would probably estimate it to be considerably lower. But if you try reading 100 words per minute (less than two words per second), you will soon put your audience to sleep, perhaps even yourself! It's a little like those slowly delivered Sunday sermons - you can hear a small chorus of snores coming from the back pews.

If we are teaching someone to read, we could look at this standard and then compare his performance to it, both in terms of his rate and errors. If he falls within the range, we could advance him to more difficult material, or we could change our strategy to see how much he understands about what he has read, which is an entirely different but equally measurable task.

If the person reads 100 words a minute one day, we could record that datum on his chart. If we continue the measurement for a minute each day, we will soon discern the rate and direction of changes in his oral reading. If his words per minute are increasing (accelerating), or his errors are decreasing (decelerating), we may continue whatever we are doing or advance him to other work. If his reading rate is not increasing or his rate of errors is not declining, we may wish to revise our approach and try something else.

The performance that is guiding our decision-making is repeatable in a fixed period of time. It can be sampled and compared with previous performances and expected levels of performance in the same way that we monitor respiration, stock charts or any other set of observable data.

Using Rate of Response as a Basic Datum

Rate is a very widely used datum in science, engineering and economics. It is equally suitable for education. We need to accomplish a major paradigm shift to allow its entry into classrooms.

If we collect frequencies over time, we can see the rate at which change is occurring. We also need to analyze the skills we are teaching into their components so that we can determine what it is we wish to measure. We could classify these skills as "tool" skills, the most fundamental ones of all. We could develop a list of "basic" and "advanced" skills.

For example, if we wish to see that students are becoming better writers, we could check out their grammar or spelling as components of their writing skills. If a student knows an "advanced" spelling rule about when to use or not to use "es" to make a word plural, we could check out his performance by providing a worksheet of words which contain examples of the rule and non-examples where adding "es" would be incorrect. We could simply ask the student to add "s" or "es" as dictated by the rule.

We already know that people can write 20-30 words or 150+ characters per minute. We could measure the student's performance for one minute, count the number of responses and chart the score. If the student wrote 150+ characters using the rule correctly, we would know that he is fluent in the use of that rule and we could move on to new curriculum.

If the student was unable to do so, we could check out the more basic skill. Do they remember the rule? When do you use "es" to make a word plural? If the student cannot determine that words ending in "ch", "sh", "s", "x", and "z" always use "es" to make them plural, he will not be able to systematically apply the rule. The "basic" skill of learning the rule and learning to distinguish examples from non-examples of the rule need remediation.

If the student could say the rule fluently and select examples and non-examples correctly, but was unable to write quickly enough, then the "tool" skill of writing characters would need to be attended to.

In any case, the teacher as diagnostician can create remedies and monitor their effectiveness by watching the rate of the student's response and the frequency of errors until the student is within the acceptable range for this skill.

The Student as Recorder

One advantage of the collection of rates of response as the basic educational datum is that the students can gather the data as reliably as the teacher. Students as young as those in Grade 1 can and have been taught to chart a number of behavioral pinpoints each day. In some cases, a team of two or three students collect the data for one another, acting as timers or counters and ensuring that the results are charted accurately on a daily basis.

In our classroom, each student typically would chart between fifteen and twenty pinpoints every day in various areas of curriculum including math, reading, reading comprehension, spelling, writing and thinking skills. Teachers and students would review their progress daily. Students were taught to bring any data which did not show growth in a three-day period to the teacher's attention. At the end of the school day, each teacher would select three students whose charts they would review in detail. Students at risk were always better represented in these selections than students who were progressing smoothly.

Human behavior does not tend to change dramatically in most instances. It is much more likely to increase or decrease at a fairly sustainable rate. Any huge changes indicated on the chart by a score well off the expected track is cause for investigation. It generally only takes a minute or two to replicate the last data.

The Acid Test

Sometimes students attempt to impress teachers with charted data points that were actually higher than their scores on the tasks. The data point would most often fall outside of the range of expected growth for one day. The teacher would simply provide another opportunity to confirm "the magnificent feat" and would see a more predictable result in a somewhat lower score. The explanation is usually one of a charting error. To err is human, to forgive divine. Even if the teacher had not caught the error, the student has now placed himself in the position of having to perform even better in subsequent measurements in order to maintain the rate of growth towards fluent performance. Students soon learn that you cannot cheat the chart.

The Student as Educational Decision Maker

When students are taught to keep and chart data on their own academic progress, they become much more involved in the learning process. Lindsley (1982) reported that children in regular elementary school classrooms increase their learning by 10% each year. Students who have data charted by their teacher grow at a rate of 20% to 40% each year. Students who are taught to chart their own progress and to be involved in decisions about improving their performance grow 80% to 100% each year.

Involving the student actively also removes much of the work from the teacher and allows the student more chance to experiment with different methods of practice or different measures of learning.

The Question of Measurement

One of the more problematic aspects of how schools currently function is the way in which they "measure" progress and report "results". Within education there is a veritable mountain of reporting systems for providing "academic" feedback to parents and kids. Some of the more common ones are reviewed in the following pages.

Anecdotal Reports

Anecdotal reports are usually written comments by the teacher intended to describe student progress without quantifying or comparing it to the performance of other students. By nature, such reports are open to a wide range of interpretation. They are often misleading and may overstate progress or understate problems. They, like all school reporting systems, are periodic and do not allow a continuous flow of information to show daily, weekly or even monthly changes in student performances. The latest trend in these reports is to computerize a data base of generic comments which the teacher selects and runs off the computer.

Anecdotal reports are favored by school authorities who do not want to attach measurement to performance for fear of hurting the child. Letting them continue on blind to their emerging lack of skills somehow seems more humane to these professionals. It would be interesting to see such advocates coach an Olympic track team using this philosophy. We might be short a Donovan Bailey or a Carl Lewis or two. I'd be more willing to gather the data and use it down to the hundredth of a second to help develop a world champion, even if on some days I had to give him some bad news about his attempts.

Letter Descriptions - E, VG, G, S, NI

Sometimes students are given letter grades which are intended to describe the quality of their performance in given academic situations. Such letter descriptions are often used in the primary grades where grading is seen to be unnecessary or even undesirable. The letters depict (E) excellent, (VG) very good, (G) good, (S) satisfactory, (NI) needs improvement.

Letter Grades A, B, C, D, E, F

Another method of grading is to assign letter grades to describe progress. This system implies some kind of equal interval scale in which 'A' is seen to be high, 'F' as a failure. Most teachers are told by the administration to never give an 'F'.

Percentage Scores

Another common system is the assignment of percentage scores. This implies that somehow the body of work represents 100% and the student has mastered x%, or that the test had 100 marks available of which the student earned a certain percentage. This is another implied scale. Closer scrutiny nearly always shows that the test was not out of 100 items, answers or even points, facts or solutions, but that the instructor derived the percentage score mathematically from the number of correct questions. In most cases, a final percentage mark is often the compilation of a set of other scores. These are sometimes scaled on a bell curve to ensure an even spread of marks from low to high across a class of students. In some cases the percent scores are then artificially raised or lowered to make them fit the "normal" curve. At this point we have come a long way from measuring what the student knows.

Count over Count Scores - 6/10

Students sometimes are awarded marks such as 6/10 on a test or exam. This can be a more finely honed description. It may actually report the number of test items and the actual number of corrects the student achieved. 5/10 is the same thing mathematically as 50%, but 50% could also mean 1 of 2 correct or 50 of 100 correct. Getting 1 out of 2 answers correct probably does not entail as much work or knowledge as getting 50 of 100 correct. But many times the denominators of a count over count measure do not correspond to the actual number of items, questions or points, but are arbitrarily assigned and therefore somewhat misleading. Most times count over count scores are transformed into a percent score, with or without being "normed" on a curve, or are reported as letter grades.

Count Over Time/Distance Scores

Count over time measures occur when the amount of time for the performance is fixed (e.g. units made per hour). Count over distance occurs when the distance is fixed (e.g. seconds in a 100 meter dash).

Once you begin using a count over time or count over distance measure, you begin to directly measure the behavior of the performer, not some abstraction of the behavior. Count over time tells us how many responses the student made in a given interval of time. It is a slightly more microscopic measure than elapsed time used in major competitions like the Olympics. In fact, in some instances the announcer will report the number of swimming strokes per minute of an Olympic swimmer and compare it to the rate of the current world record holder. At this point you get information about a count over time measure within a count over distance measure.

Count over time measures are usually found in situations where there are very great similarities between the performances of the individuals or the standard of performance involved. Count over time is most widely used in athletics when the need exists to represent small differences in performance or to measure them against a finely tuned standard. In educational settings, count over time measures exist where a specific level of performance can be stipulated, such as 30 words per minute in introductory typing, 60 words per minute for intermediate and 80 - 100 words per minute for advanced. There are very few educational situations other than typing and sports where this kind of measure is used.

Concerns with Current Educational Measurement Systems

As students and as teachers, most people have come to think of letter grades, percents and grade point averages as being a pretty normal way to measure student progress. Those who do well in elementary and secondary school tend to go on to other post secondary settings where these "measurement" systems hold sway. Teachers who go to school as part of their professional careers become familiar and at ease with these kinds of student assessment techniques. Usually they quite happily adopt them for their classrooms. There are a number of issues they tend to overlook however.

The Periodic Nature of Reporting

One of the major problems with these measures is that generally they only occur periodically. They do not provide a continuous flow of information to monitor progress. As a result, fluctuations in performance are difficult, if not impossible, to track. A student could be much more lost and experiencing increased difficulties than those indicated on the report. The measure could have been spuriously high or low because of the student's performance on that particular test day.

The Statistical Nature of the Data

Often the marks assigned to a student's performance are based on a sample of their work in a test or exam setting. The tests are then graded and marks are given. Often some composite mark from a series of tests and exams is used to derive a "final mark".

This also often introduces a statistical component to the "measurement" by using some fit to the normal curve. To adjust scores upwards or downwards, more statistics are introduced. To the extent that this happens, we become more and more removed from actual student performance and more and more involved in mathematical processes. The implication of the "normal curve" is that some people are at the top, others are in the middle and a few are at the bottom. You must compete for a display of competence in a situation where only a few can be at the top.

With actual measures of performance such as in count/time or count/distance, there is little need for statistical averaging or processing. The newest score can be directly compared to the rest of that person's scores or to those of other performers. Scores can be presented in ordinal lists from top to bottom and are directly comparable. There is room for everybody at any point of the spectrum, including the top. Olympic downhill skiing is a good example of such a performance, with the individual's best score compared with those of other skiers. There is no need to average or adjust the data.

With count over time or count over distance, the scores are completely independent of one another and it is at least theoretically possible that several individuals could achieve the same score at the very top of the distribution. People who congregate at the top are simply considered to be "fluent" in that particular behavior. A bell curve would have to be adjusted or develop a blip at the top end to show such results, rendering it less than normal.

Emphasis on Marks

Another major problem with using scores as opposed to measuring performance is that it shifts the emphasis from learning to the attainment of marks. While these two events are usually highly correlated, it does not necessarily mean that the student in fact knows the material well at all.

Robert Kiyosaki, co-founder of The Accelerated Learning Institute, cites one very good personal example of a situation where learning and marks did not necessarily correspond. As a fighter jet pilot in training as a helicopter pilot during the Vietnam war, Kiyosaki undertook advanced "gunship" training. He achieved high grades in flight school and had memorized all the necessary procedures. He relates his experience with his trainer Lt. Johnson. Lt. Johnson asked him if he knew the emergency procedures and having been answered in the affirmative, proceeded to quiz him on a few. Kiyosaki was almost insulted by the grilling. Finally Lt. Johnson allowed him to pilot the helicopter. After a few minutes, Johnson reached over, killed the engine and proceeded to look out the window as though nothing had happened. As the aircraft hurtled toward the ground, Kiyosaki's mind went blank. Finally, as the helicopter came close to crashing, Johnson took the contols, landed the helicopter, turned to Kiyosaki and said, "You won't need any Viet Cong to kill you. Your incompetence will do it for you." He then proceeded to reteach Kiyosaki using performance, not recall, so that he could land the craft with the engine off or on. Later in Vietnam, when the engine did actually fail, Kiyosaki and his crew landed the craft and survived the crash. The difference between test scores and actual performance can literally be one of life or death.

Marks are also subject to inflation when they are used as the major source of information in student selection by colleges and universities. In Canada, where a common entry exam like the Scholastic Aptitude Test is not used as a criterion for college admission, the final marks of a student's last term become critical. In the 1950s and '60s, when all students wrote a common exam that was marked independently of their school, this was not a problem. Now when schools themselves determine the marks which post-secondary institutions will use to select candidates, it does become an issue. Mark inflation creeps in as higher and higher results are needed to get into the best faculties of the best universities. Measurement becomes more elastic and less reliable.

The Empirical Basis for Using Precision Teaching

Precision Teaching was not part of Project Follow Through like the other two major technologies, Direct Instruction and Behavior Modification, used in our teaching model. It does, however, have a long and impressive empirical history of its own, including its own publication, *The Journal of Precision Teaching*, and its own international conferences and learned society.

The Empirical Data

Undoubtedly the best example of the effectiveness of Precision Teaching is to be found in its longest and most extensive study of skills development in schools - The Sacajawea Project. This project was conducted under the auspices of the U.S. Department of Education to validate the Precision Teaching model as a proven set of practices for both regular and special education settings.

The Sacajawea Project was undertaken over a twelve-year period and involved 153,000 children and 8000 teachers in 44 states and 3 Canadian provinces. Like Project Follow Through, it was a longitudinal, comparative study of methods that sought to improve student performance in basic curriculum.

As with Follow Through, standardized tests were administered to all students at the beginning and end of each year. The Sacajawea Project students were compared with students in the control groups of similar age, grade and socio-economic level. The students in the project consistently scored anywhere between 20 and 40 percentile points higher than the control groups on these independently administered tests in reading, arithmetic and spelling. They also showed better retention over time and a greater ability to transfer the use of their skills to new and more difficult tasks.

Some Advantages of Using Precision Teaching as a Universal Educational Measure

Given that every behavior has a frequency, it is possible to look at the frequency of any performance and compare it to a range of acceptable ones that define competence in that skill. Skills can be small individual components of larger skill sets or they can be more complex entities, depending on what information the teacher or learner needs to know. As long as they can be observed by either the student or the teacher, they can be counted. If they can be counted, their frequency can be determined. The change of frequency over time begins to indicate the degree of progress being made, so that adjustments can be made quickly and easily and their results seen in a short period of time.

Purity

Performances can be analyzed in a variety of ways without compressing or altering the data. The high, low and median score (the score that divides the group of scores in half) can be reported for individuals, groups of individuals within a class, an entire class, a grade level, a school, an associated group of schools, a district, region, state, national or international group.

Like individual stocks on various exchanges, they can have different starting points, different rates of acceleration or deceleration, and different values ranging from very low to very high.

The scores are directly comparable as long as we know how the information was collected and for what period of time. All of these data are on the chart.

Some Known Measures

We already know the range of frequency for some academic performances. There is still much more to be done. Everyone accepts 30 words per minute for beginning typing, 50 - 60 for intermediate and 80 - 100 for advanced. If people were more familiar with the measure, they would begin to accept 20 - 30 words per minute for handwriting, 200 - 250 words per minute for oral reading and so on. We could develop a list of the academic skills that a child should learn in each grade and a range of frequencies which would be acceptable, and begin to organize our teaching around these outcomes and standards.

The Concept of Fluency

One of the major breakthroughs of Precision Teaching is the concept of fluency developed by Eric Haughton and Carl Binder. Fluency is that level to which a skill is learned so that it is performed almost automatically and is not lost during periods of non-use. Everyone, except the most severely challenged individuals, develops a number of fluencies during his lifetime. From motor skills to verbal skills to intellectual skills, people learn to perform at fluent levels. Language is a good example.

Once we learn our mother tongue, we may be exposed to learning some other language. There is probably no easier comparison in the concept of fluency than the relative skills in first and second languages. While we can think and speak, listen and understand at fluent levels in our first language, we are relatively slow in our second language. The limitations of

134

vocabulary, the confusion of verb tenses, articles and idioms is overwhelming. Our inability to decipher speech quickly and easily, the missed words, the blank stares are all indices of the relative gap between fluent performance and beginning leanings. As we become more facile, all of these processes speed up until we finally begin thinking in our second language as we do in our mother tongue. At that point, we have become fluent. We are able to use the language quickly and easily without error and will not lose it if we don't use it for a period of time.

First Things First

Precision Teaching has attempted over the past twenty-five years to develop a list of academic fluencies, especially in core curriculum areas. These fluencies involve not only more complex skills such as decoding, but also focus on simpler tasks like saying the letters of the alphabet. These are rudimentary but essential in the learning of higher order skills. It is nearly impossible to consider doing arithmetic problems such as addition or multiplication if you have not yet learned to count. Children who have trouble in math are usually not fluent on the more basic skills. They will count using their fingers which takes much more concentration and time. Multi-step operations become very difficult, if not completely impossible to solve. They are often so focused on the counting that they make a needless error which was probably avoidable if their counting skills were automatic.

Fluent computation of basic math operations where no regrouping is involved is at 80 facts a minute. Most North American elementary students between Grades 3 and 8 do approximately 30 in addition and subtraction, fewer in multiplication and division.

Precision Teaching as an Alternative to Standardized Tests

Much of the data upon which educational decisions are

made are based on the use of standardized tests. From their first use by Alfred Binet in the Paris school system to detect low-performing students to their current use in school reform initiatives in South Carolina, Tennessee and the Dallas Independent School District among others, standardized tests have commonly been used as pre-test and post-test measures of the effectiveness of the intervention. Such tests were a part of the Follow Through research, the Sacajawea Project, Head Start and most other research attempts.

There is a host of problems with using standardized tests to make educational decisions, either for a reform initiative or for an individual child's placement. The tests are known to be unfair to minority students. They take a long time to administer and are costly. There is generally a long delay between determining the need for an assessment and the time when the results become available. In many cases, this delay is at least six months. By the time the initial request has been processed and dealt with, the child can fall almost another year behind. Standardized tests are typically given or administered by psychologists or psychometrists hired by school districts who tend to be in short supply since the educational belt-tightening of the late '80s and '90s. In situations where incentives are determined by the results of standardized test scores, there have been known cases of cheating, coaching, and outright fraud.

"Care enough to chart." - Ogden Lindsley

Precision Teaching using the Standard Celeration Chart offers a viable, inexpensive, immediate option to the use of the more cumbersome, biased, standardized tests. The behavior of a single student or of an entire class on such skills as the ability to do math calculations can literally be captured in one minute.

The measurements are unbiased in that they directly gauge the current performance of each and every student at a certain moment in time and report it as a count over time measure without statistical manipulation.

Data can be summarized by student, by classes or in any of

a multitude of ways without distorting it at all.

The use of Precision Teaching methods and the Standard Celeration Chart allows teachers to become scientific practitioners like ER technicians or ER physicians. By studying their students' responses, analyzing the effects of their interventions and making the necessary changes in time to make a difference, teachers can most efficiently employ the time and energy to impart learning.

Using Precision Teaching data from the Standard Celeration Chart, the student "tells" the teacher by his performance about the effectiveness of the teacher's instructional inputs. When the desired behavior occurs (e.g. the student is able to do more math calculations with fewer errors, read more quickly and accurately), the teacher knows that the program to teach reading decoding skills or math calculation skills is working. If the student's performance shows no change or a decrement in performance, the teacher knows that the program is not accomplishing its objectives and needs to be changed or even abandoned for one that does get results.

Precision Teaching - "A Gift from God"

Terry Harris is a 27-year-old man with an engaging smile and a tremendous sense of humor. When he was just 16-months-old, his family had little reason to laugh or, for that matter, even feel happy. Terry was diagnosed with Cerebral Palsy and the medical prognosis was dismal. Terry might talk, but it was highly unlikely that he would ever read, write or go to a regular school. He would certainly never be able to walk. It was suggested that an institution be considered.

After two days of crying, his mother, Jan, became determined to help Terry achieve his potential, whatever that might be. She started him in therapy, often driving hundreds of miles a week to his hospital sessions. At home, she worked tirelessly with him. She was sometimes criticized as expecting "too much" from her small son.

At age three, she had to stage a one-person sit-in on the front steps of a nursery school to have him accepted as a student. When he turned five, she enrolled him at a local school in the public system. She describes this year as a "Disaster with a capital 'D'". It was a lonely time for Terry. Isolated from his peers, he was placed in a corner with a tape recorder as his "teacher". His small fingers were unable to manage the machine nor the coloring activities being dictated to him. All he learned was frustration and a loathing for school. Even though he was a chatterbox at home, his teacher perceived him as "non-verbal". Since his legs wouldn't take him where he wanted to go, he escaped the agony by daydreaming. His report card at the end of the year pegged him as a "social misfit" who "didn't try". Terry summed it up best when he said in a presentation, "I can say with the deepest conviction from the pit of my soul that I attended "The Kindergarten from Hell".

Near the end of the year, Jan was summoned to a placement meeting with several school administrators. There she was introduced to Eric Haughton, a pioneer of Precision Teaching, and his wife, Elizabeth, who would be Terry's teacher in Grade 1. At the end of this meeting, Elizabeth shook Jan's hand and said, "I believe I can help your son." From that moment, they became a team on the long road to Terry's successes.

When Elizabeth first started working with Terry, he didn't know the significance of the charts she had, nor the penciled dots or even the behaviors she was measuring. He did notice, however, that she took a profound interest in the person he was. When she put her hand over his to guide him, he experienced a concern that changed school for him from misery to new hope. If he tuned out half-way through a one-minute timing, Eric would gently say, "You're being timed, my friend", and back into reality he would come. Daydreaming was no longer required as an escape. Terry soon saw that genuine learning was taking place. Eric was a master at extinguishing unhealthy behaviors and will always be remembered for his conviction that new behaviors represented new learning.

Terry started to learn the value of setting aims and goals. During the two years under Elizabeth's tutelage, they worked on anywhere from 5 to 25 charts at any one time. There was a lot of modeling, a lot of coaching and loads of practice. When he became fluent at making straight marks in small boxes, he learned how to print his name. Eventually he could print words and then stories.

Near the end of Grade 1, Elizabeth suggested to Jan that Terry leave his crutches behind in the classroom when he left for a weekend. She thought he functioned better without them and she wanted to see how well he could manage on his own. Terry learned to walk. After much practice, he could climb stairs and even swim. At age 10, on Eric's suggestion, he began to learn to ski. For six years, the family traveled five hours to a mountain where Terry at first picked himself up every ten feet. He was eventually able to manage continuous runs down the slopes.

Another huge accomplishment was his graduation from Velcro shoes to normal ones when, at age 17, he learned to tie his laces. A few years later, with a pair of tightly laced Reebok runners and a tough-minded optimism, he completed a 10 kilometer Terry Fox Run in his hometown of Belleville.

Terry graduated from high school and obtained a B.A. from Brock University in Ontario. He is presently working towards his Masters of Divinity in counseling at Tyndale Seminary in Toronto. He drives a 1991 Suzuki Sidekick around the city and has a wonderful young lady as a fiancee, who, like Eric, Elizabeth and his parents, is committed to helping Terry learn new behaviors. He is a popular motivational speaker at universities, colleges, medical functions and conferences.

Terry Harris' 27 years are full of remarkable accomplishments. His successes, which he sees as journeys rather than destinations, have never come easily. He has had to be persistent, determined and directed. Without Precision Teaching and some caring mentors in his early years, he could have traveled down a totally different road than the one he is on today. In his own words, Terry says, "It would be inaccurate to say that I attribute all my success to Precision Teaching. This would be excluding the participation of a merciful God, a supportive family and a dedicated team. I would say that P.T. is an answer to prayer. It is a buried treasure, the value of which can only be known within the context of the loving relationships which I have been privileged to experience."

Summary

Precision Teaching with its development of the Standard Celeration Chart provides a completely new measurement dimension to gauge educational performance and set educational standards. It avoids many of the complications foisted upon the teaching profession by standardized tests or other less exact forms of reporting student achievement.

Its history contains strong empirical support from research in classes from kindergarten through university.

Precision Teaching provides daily hard data using frequency and rate in an easily readable form equivalent to the data used in science and economics and accessed every day by millions of individuals interested in tracking their investments. It has proven its effectiveness in classrooms across North America, but continues to be almost completely unused by either school administrators or classroom teachers. Its adoption will require a significant paradigm shift from the conventional procedures of today in which our schools ignore any form of continuous data on student performance.

Directed and
Independent Practice

• •

"Knowledge is a treasure but practice is the key to it."
- Thomas Fuller

What is it?

Directed Practice

Directed practice is that which is monitored by the teacher as the student performs. It's usually part of the lesson or done shortly after the lesson as seatwork. Directed practice is intended to reduce errors quickly by providing feedback, direction and any necessary corrections so that the student begins doing the task correctly. This type of practice will continue until the student has shown the ability to do the task independently without a high-error frequency. Directed practice typically does not require inordinate amounts of the teacher's time. The lion's share of the time a student spends practicing is done on his own.

Independent Practice

Independent practice should consume at least 50% of all of the time dedicated to teaching. Practice is crucial and needs to be given the time and attention it requires to learn skills to fluent levels of performance.

The Direct Instruction programs are a good example of the role of practice in instruction. If you analyze them on a lesson-by-lesson basis across any of the programs, you quickly notice that they have a substantial amount of directed practice in the early part of program, and relatively little independent practice. After a few lessons, independent practice is increased, with directed practice only on the new tasks. Gradually the independent practice increases to become the bulk of the lesson as previously taught skills are reintroduced on a continuous review basis.

As students work through the program, the amount of instruction decreases as the amount of practice increases, gradually turning over much of the responsibility to the students to continue to practice skills they already know, but in which they have yet to become fluent.

Timed Practice

In the use of Precision Teaching, students are often given the opportunity for timed practices. Academic measures on such topics as oral reading, writing math facts, naming states/countries on a national or international map can be used to continuously track the progress of the student on a specific pinpoint.

If students are charting their daily progress on the Standard Celeration Chart, they may choose to record either all of their scores as a stack of dots or their best score for that particular day as a single dot.

Timed practices provide immediate feedback as opposed to simply finishing a worksheet or an assigned exercise which is handed in to be marked later by the teacher. Timed practices also tell students how far their current performance is from the expected range for that particular task. They allow students to reach personal daily goals on their journey to more distant accomplishments. They signal deficiencies and roadblocks to progress and allow for analysis and prescription by the teacher and/or student. Often that will mean changing the task, perhaps changing the input or output channel that the student is using to practice the task.

Learning Channels

Humans are highly visual organisms. A large proportion of the sensory information they use involves vision. They use their entire set of sensory receptors including hearing, touch, smell and position to constantly monitor their world. In analyzing learning, it is generally helpful to pay attention to the type of sensory input and the verbal, motor or other output the student is employing to learn a concept or the application of some concept or operation. Taking the input and output channels together generates learning channel pairs. Some tasks may be more quickly or easily learned when a specific learning channel pair is used.

For example, when students read aloud, they see the words and then say them. Thus the learning channel is "see/say words". This designation is useful in practicing with any student. If the learning channel has been specified, as opposed to simply saying "reading", the person monitoring the practice has a more detailed idea of how to do the practice and how it has been done in the past.

Changing the input or output of the learning channels changes the task. If the student has been writing the answers to basic math computations and you switch to having him touch the problem and say the answer, you would generally see changes in the student's performance. Sometimes by varying the input or output channel, the student can begin to achieve again when practice has hit a snag.

A few ranges of desired performance using learning channels for oral reading and arithmetic are listed below as examples. All pinpoints assume no more than 2 errors per minute as an accuracy criterion. These fluency levels are independent of grade, sex, age, race, socio-economic status, etc.

Reading:
- See/Say sounds in isolation   60 - 80 sounds/minute
- See/Say single words in lists   80 - 100 words/minute
- Think/Say alphabet in order   300 - 400 letters/minute
- See/Say sound out words   20 - 30 words/minute
- See/Say words in sentences   200+ words/minute

- See/Think words in context   400 - 500 words/minute
- Think/Say ideas from reading   20 - 30 ideas/minute
- Think/Write facts from story   20 - 30 facts/minute

Arithmetic:
- Hear/Write numbers (random)   80 - 100 numbers/minute
- Think/Write numbers in sequence 120 - 160 numbers/minute
- See/Say numbers (random)   80 - 100 numbers/minute
- See/Write math facts   80 - 100 facts/minute
  (single digit problems)

Once students reach these levels of fluency, the skill will remain available to them with only occasional practice. It's a little like riding a bike - if you do it often enough to become a proficient cyclist as a child, you will still be able to ride as an adult even after years without practice. When you start back after extended periods of absence, your performance may be a little shaky, but it does return quickly to its old patterns.

In 1977, Eric Haughton and I collected data on students in Grade 4 classrooms in the Hastings County Board of Education. We had them do a single See/Say Story timing for one minute. We recorded their scores and the students went off on their nine-week summer break. In September we returned to the same students and had them do the task again. Students who had been fluent were able to perform at their previous levels. Students who were reading fewer than 200 words per minute, read fewer words with more errors than they had in June. Students with the lowest frequencies suffered the greatest losses in reading on returning to school. 200+ words per minute seems to be a level at which students are less likely to lose their reading decoding skills without routine practice.

An Example of Timed Practice to Increase Expressive Writing Production

Teachers of English often complain of the poor work pupils produce when they are given in-class writing assignments. With some students, even after 10 - 15 minutes, there is little or nothing to show for their efforts. They typically complain that they can't think of anything to write. We used the following timed procedure to increase expressive writing output to fluent levels of 20 - 30 words per minute:

1. The students are asked to select a topic or are given a topic.
2. There is a one-minute timing in which the students write as many ideas about the topic they can think of.
3. There is a second one-minute timing in which they organize their ideas by listing them in the order in which they will write about them. This could be by numbering the ideas on the list or actually rewriting the listed ideas in order of importance, chronology or in some other order they intend to use.
4. The next step is a five-minute timing to write a beginning draft.
5. The final step is a one-minute timing to edit for spelling, punctuation, subject-verb agreement and so on.
6. Finally the draft is rewritten in good and handed in.

Once students can write 120 - 150 words, edited and submitted for review, they can select a new topic. If students have difficulty, the same exercise is done the next day, using their existing copy as a guide. Generally a project can be completed in two to three days. As with other practice, each effort starts with a little better initial score than the last attempt.

This exercise can be used for major assignments where each section of the paper is treated as a mini-project and done using the above format. In cases where students have difficulties generating ideas, pictures can be used to help develop their list of ideas to write about. Prompts can be given, such as telling what is happening in the picture, what might have preceded and what might happen next. Such timed exercises can provide the framework to get performance to levels where it yields enough output for the teacher and student to work with. It is practically impossible to create writers when there is little or no production. The idea of timed story writing is to increase the volume of writing so that you have something to critique.

Practice - The Key to Excellence

Every teacher and every coach knows the importance of practice. Practice generally follows the 80-20 rule. You can get about 80% of the effect in 20% of the practice. The last 20% requires 80% of the practice to attain. Watching Mary Lou Retton or Elvis Stojko or any world-class athlete is a testament to practice. As teachers, we have to select the topics of greatest importance to practice so that the most critical skills are the ones our students learn best.

Anne Desjardins, co-author of the journal article on the integration of the QLC learning model, worked with severely handicapped children before coming to our school. These children were unable to walk, feed themselves, dress, toilet or do many of the things normal children learn to do at an early age. Anne introduced what became known as THE BIG SIX. THE BIG SIX are the rudimentary tool skills from which more complex skills are built. They are POINT, REACH, TOUCH, GRASP, TURN and RELEASE. Some combination of these skills is critical to being able to feed yourself, open a door, put on a sock and do the everyday things most of us take for granted.

Anne taught each of these skills independently, aiming for a child to be able to point at, reach, grasp and release objects and to make a wrist turning motion, all at 100 per minute. Once her handicapped charges had learned these tool skills to fluent levels of performance, she began to combine them into more complex patterns to teach other tasks like feeding. The child would point his hand in the direction of the spoon, reach for it, grasp it, point it toward the bowl of soup, and so on until he was feeding himself independently. The training required a lot of prompts and physical hand-over-hand guiding, but gradually the children learned and became increasingly skillful. The learning required such masses of practice and the gains were so small on a daily basis that they were not obvious until they were charted over weeks and months. Only then did the increased performance show itself in the data. More concretely, Anne had these children walking, toileting, feeding, dressing themselves and going off to class in a school outside of the facility within two years. The practice of simple skills to fluent levels was the key to learning more complex skills which ultimately allowed these children much greater freedom and a better quality of life.

Fluent Frees and Threes (A Case Study)

With quick steps to the right, left, forwards and back, Kim Graf fires shot after shot at the hoop. The standing-room-only crowd roars its approval with each successful basket. Her opponent tries to keep up the pace, and the announcer, gasping for breath, barely manages to maintain a running commentary of the action.

This scene occurred night after night in the basement of the Graf family home in Poland, Ohio, as three-year-old Kim developed her basketball shooting skills. She shot three balls of foam rubber about the size of a volleyball. The basket - one step up from John Naismith's peach bucket - consisted of a plastic hoop with a small backboard of plexiglas that had replaced the worn-out cardboard original. The pole, of mini height, was also made of cardboard.

The frenzy of the crowd was cranked out by Kim's dad, Steve, when he emitted an encouraging "aaaahhhh" in a way that represented thousands of cheering fans. Her father also played the simultaneous roles of the ragged opponent and the breathless commentator. The game was always fast-paced and featured its own rules - lots of shooting from a variety of spots in one-minute timed halves.

As Kim grew, so did the height of the net. Foam balls were replaced by regular basketballs and practices were moved from the basement to school gymnasiums. The constant was that the emphasis of every practice remained on speed, with only an occasional tinkering with form and technique. The timings were always done with at least two balls, so that the shooter was in perpetual motion. Results were charted. The data showed a continuous climb for successful shots in a one-minute time period.

So who is this Steve Graf, you might ask? A former NBA

giant who hooked on to his daughter's rising star? A University coach? An Olympic trainer? None of the above. Steve Graf holds a Ph.D. from Ohio State and is currently a professor of Psychology at Youngstown State University. He was trained by Ogden Lindsley, the father of Precision Teaching, and instruction in charting fluencies on the Standard Celeration Chart is an integral part of his course curriculum.

The rapid, two to three ball practice method was suggested by Lindsley to Kim's dad. Over the span of two decades, it has reaped huge benefits for Kim and her family.

At age 13, she won an international free-throw competition, making all of her 28 shots. She set records in free-throws, three-pointers and scoring at Poland High School during her four years there. She won a scholarship to attend Kenyon College in Gambier, Ohio. By the time she was a senior there, their women's basketball team had gone from a two-win season the year before Kim graduated from high school to a impressive 26-2 standing. They won their first ever women's basketball championship, both for regular and tournament play in Kim's last year. In NCAA stats for three-pointers made per game, she ranked among the top four in the U.S. for each of her four years at college, leading the nation in Division III as a senior. She wound up her ball career with a total of 365 three-point shots, the second highest total in women's basketball history. If all that isn't enough to knock your Nikes off, the combination of basketball and academic fluency helped Kim to earn some $96,000 in scholarships over her four-year college career!

Obviously practice played a major role in Kim's tremendous success as a basketball player. Their best guess as to the key feature leading to fluency was the focus on speed. A shooter who takes time to think what to do prior to each practice shot may never develop the automatic same-every-time advantage afforded high-frequency practice. One learns to be accurate by monitoring what parts of form make a difference. This seems easier to do when practice occurs at high speed.

One might speculate that Kim is simply a gifted athlete whose practice regimen was secondary in her accomplishments. Not so. There are two other sisters on the Graf team who are showing the same promise. Using a similar three-point shooting strategy, Allison and Steffi are both playing to the cheers of the crowds. (And not just Dad's "aaaahhhhhs"!) The former has broken her older sister's high school 3-point records as a 9th, 10th and 11th grader. Her 11th grade total broke the all-time school record Kim set as a senior. Interestingly, Allison, who has not followed the speed prescription in her free-throw practice, has not exceeded Kim's 83% career achievement.

Steffi, the youngest hoopster, connected on several three-pointers in games as a 6th grader. The summer before she started 7th grade, she made 25 3's in a three-minute practice timing. Her future looks bright.

Fluency in frees and threes? The Graf girls are proof positive. Practice does make perfect.

SAFMEDS

Another method of practice developed by Ogden Lindsley are SAFMEDS, a timed version of flashcards. SAFMEDS is an acronym for "Say All Facts a Minute Each Day". The object is to have students practice and measure their mastery of the material contained on the cards in a one-minute daily measurement. Much of the recent work on SAFMEDS has been done by Steve Graf (1994) at Youngstown University. He is trying to spread the technology with templates, a how-to book and workshops.

SAFMEDS are decks of cards printed front and back. The front could be a concept with the back being a definition. Or the front could be a math fact with the answered problem written on the back. SAFMEDS are limited to 50 cards because that's about the number an individual can handle easily in a minute.

SAFMEDS serve to help learners achieve fluency on a content area. They illustrate to students what information needs to be learned and how well it is to be learned. They can use different learning channels, but will usually rely on the

See/Say combination.

During a course he was teaching at the University of Kansas, Ogden Lindsley asked his students to define terms needed for the course. He found that they were slow and made errors. Lindsley provided them with a list of terms and the definitions for each and had them create SAFMEDS for the lexicon of the course. As part of the final evaluation, each student met with Lindsley, handed him the deck of cards which Lindsley shuffled and handed back. Then in one minute, the student would look at a card, see the word and say the definition to Lindsley, who kept track of any errors or skips. If the student was fluent, i.e. could repeat definitions at 20 - 30 per minute, Lindsley was satisfied that he could "talk the talk". If he was not fluent, he simply went home and practiced until he was in the fluent range of performance on terms used in the course.

In order to be sure they were inside the range of fluency, students would accelerate their speaking rate. Once a colleague of Lindsley happened by the door while one of the students was well into a one-minute timing and speaking at a faster than normal rate. He shook his head and walked on, convinced that Ogden was catching hell from one of his students.

Practice Sheets

In today's more laissez-faire approach to education which has dominated classrooms for the past thirty years, the role of practice has been denigrated and downplayed. Creativity has been elevated to new heights, but often not clearly defined as to how students become so or how teachers provide for it.

Skill building through practice was largely written off as "drill and kill", meaning that it was boring, demotivating and killed any opportunity for creativity. It is only now, after 30 years of declining S.A.T. scores, dropping performances on international tests, growing rates of illiteracy and innumeracy and their related financial and human costs, that we are prepared to challenge the open classroom, creativity-based learning and student-centered teaching approaches. The data from centers like QLC, Morningside, Ben Bronz and others who have chosen a more empirical approach further strengthens our argument (see Part Five). Although practice may at times be unglamorous and even tedious, it is necessary in large amounts to build skills.

Various states and provinces are now requiring more practice as part of the outcomes for reforming their schools. New York State, for example, now demands that students in elementary schools practice their reading by completing twenty-five books per year. They are expected to write 1000 words of prose per month and do an assigned amount of math. Much of this emphasis on productivity is aimed at increasing the practice of fundamental academic skills that will impact the literacy issues these schools are currently facing.

The traditional worksheets of math facts, spelling, grammar and other areas of curriculum are experiencing a resurgence. A skillful teacher can sequence such practice to ensure that each newly taught skill has accompanying practices. These can be used as seatwork for some groups while others are being taught. They can also be used as the basis for daily data collection so that the results can be charted and decisions made about the next step in that curriculum for any student.

The practice sheets also benefit from better instructional design. They can now cover the entire range of examples that are taught by a Direct Instruction teaching presentation. They can include both examples and non-examples of the concept, operation, application or rule in question.

One problem with practice sheets is that there can be an effect on performance due to the constant order that the items appear. One option is to number the items and start at a different number each time. Steve Graf (1989) and his colleagues at Zero Bros. Software created a computer program called *PracticeSheeter* to create worksheets which automatically randomize the items before each printing.

Summary

Once the instruction is completed, practice is the difference between becoming skillful, remaining mediocre or forgetting altogether. Despite the attacks on repetitious practicing, there remains little question as to its value in building skills. Coaches, especially at competitive levels, understand its role. Educators often do not.

The QLC model integrated learning outcomes, behavior management, Direct Instruction, Precision Teaching and practice ~ all powerful teaching components which, when combined, result in highly effective instruction.

Part Five will outline the implementation of this basic model at Quinte Learning Center, followed by a review of its successful use by a number of practitioners with different populations of children and adults across North America.

Part Five

· ·

Applications
of the Model

Integrating The Technologies and Creating Synergy

"Acting on a good idea is better than just having a good idea."
- Robert Half

Quinte Learning Center Ltd. / QLC Educational Services Inc. / CyberSlate Corporation (Belleville, Ontario, Canada) - Michael Maloney, Founder

When the Quinte Learning Center grew into a full-time private day school registered with the Ontario Ministry of Education, it presented the author and his staff with the first opportunity to use the QLC model for the entire curriculum with a group of students at risk of school failure. The original presentation of its research was a symposium featured at the Association for Behavior Analysis conference in Milwaukee, Wisconsin, in 1982. It is also fully documented in a journal article by Maloney, Desjardins and Broad, a publication from which this book gained its title.

Although the day-school program was discontinued in favor of developing the educational computer software programs, *Mighty Math* and *Math Tutor*, the model continued to be used with thousands of tutorial and summer-school clients, both children and adults. The data presented here were replicated in each of the three years in which the day school operated.

The School

The Quinte Learning Center school was housed in Queen

Mary School, a centrally located Hastings County Board of Education building which had been deemed surplus. It was also home to a ballet school, an arts council, a group of painters, and a child-care program. We had two classrooms, the second being used for our adult program and for after-school tutorials.

The Clients

For each of the three years, the clients consisted of approximately twenty children from the city of Belleville and the surrounding area who were at risk of school failure. They had been registered in various local schools in placements from Grade 2 to Grade 8 and ranged in age from seven to fourteen. Most of them were two to three years behind their peers in school. Every year the makeup of the class changed as children returned to the local school system. Generally there was a three-to-one ratio of males to females.

The Teachers

The staff consisted of a principal, two full-time teachers and some part-time teachers. Neither Anne Desjardins nor Pam Broad were certified teachers, but had come from Loyalist College's Human Sciences programs. Lynne Brearley, a local teacher, taught the children French, as all Ontario students are enrolled in French at least until high school. We wanted to ensure that our students were as competent as any other students in their study of a second language.

The other part-time teachers were working artists - potters, stained glass makers and painters - who taught their specialty to the children during their weekly art periods. The class would visit the artists' premises to fire their clay, cut their glass, etc. Physical education concentrated on teaching activities that could be played for a lifetime. Instruction was given in soccer, swimming, squash and softball. A local motel provided the pool, while a nearby fitness club made squash courts available for a modest fee. Students acted as custodians to help clean the classrooms every day. Each had a job from a job bank that changed every month.

The Program

The program was constructed from the individual parts of the model, drawn together to create a strong and integrated curriculum. It contained behavioral objectives, classroom management, Direct Instruction, Precision Teaching, and directed and independent practice regimens.

The school's program was highly academic, concentrating on the basics - reading, reading comprehension, spelling, grammar, writing skills, arithmetic, physical education, art, and French. Time was also scheduled at the local library to teach library skills. Field trips and other outings were included to give the students a full range of activities, like those of the schools they had left and to which they would likely return.

Each day consisted of 30 to 40-minute periods for each of the subjects listed above. The Direct Instruction Corrective and Mastery series of programs were used for all areas of study except French, art and physical education. The objective of each day was to cover at least one lesson in each subject area, so that every student would complete at least one year's program within one year.

Students were divided into small groups with similar academic needs. These groups changed as students progressed or needed additional remediation. Since the Direct Instruction Corrective and Mastery series of programs provide a continuum of lessons spanning several grade levels in each subject area, it was possible to place the students at some point in the continuum in any subject and then move them forward at least one complete level. Such progress would constitute a full year's course.

The Contract

Each parent or set of parents signed a written contract with the school. The contract contained provision for the amount and timing of tuition payments, the transportation of the student to and from the school and other housekeeping matters like attendance, holidays, etc. The contract also committed the school to achieve at least a year's academic progress as measured by commonly accepted standardized tests with each child, regardless of the current academic difficulties or diagnosed learning problems they were said to have. It outlined the classroom rules and obliged the parents to support the efforts of the teachers by accepting and cooperating with the school's code of conduct.

The contract also involved the parents in a monthly meeting at the school. This was a pot-luck dinner held on the third Thursday of each month to which all members of the students' families were invited. Each family contributed a dish from an assigned food list. Sometimes grandmothers or visiting relatives would show up to see what we were doing. After the meal, a monthly student progress report was given to all in attendance. The meeting was held to outline the students' data, discuss any problems or concerns, celebrate achievements and prepare for the next month. Individual meetings with parents were held on an as-needed basis.

The Results

Each year the students were tested using the same standardized tests used by the local board. This was done to ensure results would be accepted by the local schools to which these students would return. The results were also used in our research for those educators who were unaware or skeptical of Precision Teaching data. The Canadian Test of Basic Skills and the Wide Range Achievement Test were administered at the beginning and end of each year. The results showed an average growth of 2.4 years for each student during each year of study.

This became even more significant when compared to those children who remain in North American special-education classrooms. On average, these students gain only .7 of a year during each academic year. Our students, most of whom also came from "special-education" classrooms, were surpassing 2.4 years, more than three and a half times the progress of their public school peers. In comparison to regular classroom students, their growth was nearly two and a half times greater. These results were consistent for students across the three years of the program.

The Internal Daily Measures

Equally interesting was the daily student data. Everyone was taught to chart daily progress on a wide range of academic pinpoints using the Standard Celeration Chart. On any given day, the students would practice ten to twelve topics in the various subject areas they were studying. Typically, they would complete two or three topics in arithmetic, one or two in decoding (reading), two or three in reading comprehension, a couple in spelling, writing and perhaps some tool skills like counting. Each day they would practice and then measure and chart their frequencies for each of these skills. If their performance improved, they would move on to the next topic. If their performance reached the standard that was set for that behavior, they would start a new exercise, such as practicing the use of a new spelling rule. If their performance did not change, they would try a variety of strategies to increase their correct responses or reduce their errors. If, after three days of attempts, they were unable to see improvement, they would bring their data to the teacher and work out an intervention plan.

The teachers would check the students' charts throughout the day and assist with practice and decision-making. The continuous flow of data allowed the students and teachers to see the progress, the problems, the decisions and their immediate effects. It involved the students in the decisions about their learning and what was or what was not working at any particular time. It pointed out the need to develop strong tool skills like counting or writing digits, so that they could aim for more complex academic tasks. Both the frequency of correct answers and the frequency of errors were important data, each affecting the decision as to what to do next.

The data on common pinpoints were summarized monthly and presented at the monthly parent meeting. Each of the students' scores for the day before the meeting would be recorded. The range of scores and the median would be determined and matched against the known standard for that particular task (e.g. 200+ words per minute in oral reading). Parents could then compare their child's performance to both the individual's scores over the previous months and the data from the entire class on the same task.

The parents were also taught how to use the Standard Celeration Chart so that they could make sense of the data being kept by their son(s) or daughter(s). As part of the monthly school meeting, the students would review with their parent(s) the work they had charted during the past month, the goals they had met, the number of new tasks they had been able to add to their program, and any changes they and their teachers had made to their program.

Adult Literacy

Almost from the inception of the Quinte Learning Center, adult students were part of the mix. Social agencies sought us out and enrolled their illiterate clients. Usually these individuals would attend on a daily basis for three hours, and would be studying the same basic literacy and numeracy courses as the younger students. As with the parents, we arranged a contract with the social worker and the client which outlined each party's responsibility.

Most of our adult clients were eager to learn the skills that would make them eligible for training and would free them from social-welfare agencies. A very few were attempting a free ride on the social-service system. The results reflected the differences very clearly. Those adult students who attended daily, who were punctual and completed their assignments were uniformly successful. Those who were prone to absenteeism, lateness and whose dog ate their homework did not fare well. We attempted to differentiate the two types at the earliest possible moment. Approximately 15% of our adult clients were malingerers. We would deal with the situation in the contract. The first month was a no-fault opportunity for everyone to try the program. If anyone - the client, the social worker or the teacher - was dissatisfied, the contract ended with no penalties to anyone. Once the second month began, all of the cards were on the table. If the teacher failed, we did not get paid. If the client was absent, late or unwilling to complete his assignments, he was removed from the program and in many cases, his vocational rehabilitation stipend was discontinued.

As with the full-day students, the data were carefully kept and reported to the client and the agency on a monthly basis (or immediately if there was a problem) so that there were no surprises. Despite repeated warnings and whatever additional help we offered to our difficult clients, we still lost approximately 10% of our adult agency-sponsored students because they refused to abide by their contracts. The agencies were concerned by the loss of opportunity for these individuals but they were also relieved at not having to support those who were unwilling to attend, arrive for class on time or do the assigned work.

The Workers' Compensation Board Clients

In September of 1991, a vocational rehabilitation caseworker from the Workers' Compensation Board came to the Quinte Learning Center's Belleville operation. His client, an injured worker named Clyde, needed literacy skills to start the retraining program which would enable him to work in some role other than that of forklift operator. Clyde could only recognize a few simple words. The caseworker asked if we could teach the man to read and, if so, how long it would take. After a quick analysis of Clyde's almost non-existent reading skills, I told the worker that we could teach Clyde to read at a Grade six level in two months, if he could come every morning for three hours.

After he picked himself up off the floor, the caseworker came as close to calling me a liar as he could without being unprofessional. I simply showed him the final lesson Clyde would be reading when the two months were over. I told him that Clyde would read 200 words per minute with no more than two errors per hundred words. I then asked him to enroll Clyde and in two months to check on his progress. If it was lacking, he simply did not need to pay the account. He agreed.

Because of his injury, Clyde often worked in great discomfort and was frequently whacked out by the necessary painkillers. Despite this, he was heroic in his efforts. He sometimes read in a prone position because it was the only way to help control his back pain. His injuries were so extensive and permanent that he was never permitted to attend retraining, but at the end of eight weeks, we lived up to our word and our bill was paid. Clyde had learned to read, write and spell well enough to become a literate person.

A Major Breakthrough

At the end of his second month, Clyde read his first novel. He selected Farley Mowat's *Two For The North*, which he enjoyed immensely. He even took it to read to his mother on his next visit to Newfoundland. He could hardly wait to show her how well he was learning. A few weeks later, Farley Mowat just happened to be in Belleville at a literary arts function. Learning of Clyde and his valiant fight to become a reader, he sent him a signed copy of his best-known book, *Never Cry Wolf*. Some things can make you feel very proud. This was one such moment for me.

Expansion

As a result of our success with Clyde, other Workers' Compensation Board caseworkers began to send us clients, first to Belleville, then increasingly to our other four locations across the province. The company expanded to a total of ten sites, adding a high-school upgrading program and an English as a Second Language course. Soon we had more than 350 injured workers enrolled.

The caseworkers appreciated the contracts and the reporting relationship between the center's manager and themselves. Students no longer spent months in courses where no information came back to the agency regarding their progress or attendance. The fact that we would terminate clients for truancy or not completing their assigned work brought a degree of accountability which they had not achieved with local colleges, school boards, or literacy agencies.

In fact, the process worked so well that we began receiving clients who had been a part of the vocational rehabilitation caseload for a long time and had shown little or no progress in a series of retraining placements. The contract resolved the problem by either changing their attitude and teaching them to be good students or by having them terminated with little hope of future funding.

Many Happy Endings, A Few Sad Ones

Over 90% of our Workers' Compensation Board clients successfully completed their programs on time and to the expected levels. Some were unable to complete their studies because of the extent of their injury and were referred for medical rehabilitation. For a few, the program was too demanding, given the time available for retraining. Some were malingerers who refused to honor their contracts and were terminated. In many cases, because we are a registered private secondary school, we were able to recommend that the Ministry of Education and Training award the student his secondary school diploma.

The most important set of data, however, relates to the success of the clients who left the Quinte Learning Center to become enrolled in a community college program. Over ninety percent of those students successfully completed their first semester of college.

We Grow

As the company grew and expanded to ten centers across the province of Ontario, and our successes became known, colleagues visited the Quinte Learning Center. They adopted and adapted the model to meet the needs of their emerging learning centers which began to appear across North America since the early eighties. Their stories follow in Chapter 12.

The
Expansion Teams

* *

"If you have knowledge, let others light their candle by it."
- Margaret Fuller

The following stories are told in the chronological order in which my colleagues developed their enterprises. Each center, although emanating from the same basic model, is as different as its founder and the needs and demands of its environment.

Morningside Learning Center / Morningside Academy / Morningside Learning Systems (Seattle, Washington) - Kent Johnson, Founder

In the summer of 1981, Kent Johnson made the trek from the state of Washington to Belleville to visit the Quinte Learning Center. He had heard of us and was interested in setting up a similar business in Seattle. Later that year, he founded Morningside Learning Center and with the help of Anne Desjardins soon had a second Morningside site in Bellingham. The centers grew and became a full-time school which was renamed Morningside Academy.

Like Quinte, Morningside was developed to provide behaviorally designed academic and social programs for children. It is a state-approved private school which provides a money-back guarantee of two years' progress for each year the student is enrolled. During the six-week summer session, a guarantee of one year of progress in the area of greatest deficit is promised.

The Students

The Academy enrolls students from ages five to eighteen in kindergarten through 12th grade. Some are diagnosed as "learning disabled" (LD), others are labeled "attention deficit hyperactivity disorder" (ADHD). Many have no specific label, but are behind at school. Some have social and/or familial problems as well as academic deficits. According to Kent, "Morningside Academy students perform below their potential in school because of either: a) deficient basic academic skills such as reading, writing and mathematics, b) deficient learning skills such as listening, noticing, thinking, studying, and organizing, and/or c) deficient performance skills in completing tasks in a timely, accurate and organized manner, without disrupting others or causing oneself undue grief." Students attend Morningside Academy for periods of one to four years before returning to public schools.

The Process

Each student is enrolled in structured programs. After successfully completing the instructional part of the lesson, the student does timed practices on a variety of pinpoints to strengthen new learning and reach fluent levels of performance.

Timings are generally one minute, but can range from 10 seconds for some highly repetitive task like counting, to 10 minutes for a writing task. Students chart their own results and indicate to a teacher when they are ready to change curriculum or are in need of assistance. Practice is spaced and cumulative for best effects.

The Results

Over the past ten years that Morningside Academy has operated its full-time day school, its students have averaged gains of 2.5 years for every year they were enrolled (Johnson, 1998). The summer schools have consistently raised the academic skills of the student one full year during an intensive remedial course in one curriculum area such as reading or math. Although the bulk of the students have thick files of educational and psychological testing and have been diagnosed as learning disabled or hyperactive, student progress is highly impressive. Per year of enrollment between 1981 and 1992, the children's mean standardized test score in reading shows a gain of two and a half years, language arts approaches a four-year gain and mathematics is crossing the three-year growth mark. Equally importantly, the students continue to do well when they return to public schools. When Kent, his staff and his students fix the problem, it stays fixed.

Morningside Innovations

The TAPS Program

Kent Johnson and his associates are observant behavioral researchers using a steady stream of performance data. They have devised additional methods to facilitate their students' learning which are not found in the original model. The TAPS (Talk Aloud Problem Solving) program assists students by having them focus on how to think by talking their way through new problems in reading comprehension, mathematics, social studies and science. This is not free-association blabbering, but a highly organized series of strategies modeled by their teachers to solve specific problems in efficient ways.

Morningside Learning Systems

In 1995, Kent Johnson and Hollind Kevo, his 10-year associate in the development of Morningside Academy, founded Morningside Learning Systems. It is a training and consulting company that brings the Morningside Model to elementary school districts. The district's teachers are trained to teach, assess and place students in the Morningside reading, writing, mathematics and content programs. The plan also includes individual teacher coaching on a monthly basis, demonstrating effective strategies during actual instructional periods and guiding practice of the methods.

Training for new teachers, ongoing workshops for Morningside teachers, consultation with principals and district personnel, train-the-trainer sessions and other strategies are employed to ensure the expansion and self-maintenance of the program.

This training arm of Morningside has successfully implemented in-school programs for children and adults in the Nechako District of British Columbia, the Seattle, as well as the Chicago Public Schools.

In each case the students' learning doubled each year. The Chicago schools were in such jeopardy that Mayor Richard Daley simply took them over and hired Kent Johnson, Joe Layng and others, including Zig Engelmann, to come in and clean them up. These were schools where not a single child enrolled had shown any growth on any measure for an entire year.

In 1997, the 23rd Conference for the Association for Behavior Analysis, of which all of these behavioral educators are members, was held in the downtown Chicago Hilton Hotel. Conference participants woke up one morning to a photo of Mayor Richard Daley on the front page of the *Chicago Tribune*. He was standing in front of one of Morningside's Chicago schools. Daley publicly announced that all Chicago schools should look like this one. The academic results that were expected due to Morningside's intervention had been attained earlier than expected and had drawn the attention of the chief city administrator and the journalists.

The Summer School Institute

Each summer for the past six years Morningside Learning Systems has presented its annual Summer Institute. Teachers can learn about its data-driven behavioral approach which guarantees and delivers two years of growth in one. From late July to mid-August, teachers can involve themselves in almost 200 hours of extensive training and application of new methods. The Institute provides two strands of programs - The Morningside Model of Generative Instruction and The

Overview of Instructional Design.

The former includes training on classroom management practices, Direct Instruction, fluency building, Precision Teaching, peer coaching, the TAPS program, curriculum decisions, as well as evaluation and selection of basic skills curriculum. The second strand is an overview and a survey of instructional design principles. It shows teachers how to analyze the instructional content of their existing programs and how to write sequences of tasks in Direct Instruction and programmed text formats. Designing effective practice materials and empirically validating the materials with real performance data are also an integral part of the course.

Daily hands-on practice for both programs is provided with children enrolled in the Morningside Summer School so that teachers can actually see the methods at work.

The Learning Incentive / Ben Bronz Academy / CyberSlate Corp. (West Hartford, Connecticut) - Ian Spence and Aileen Stan-Spence, Founders

Located in West Hartford, Connecticut since 1982, The Learning Incentive is a private agency devoted to intensive remedial education. It currently has four divisions: Ben Bronz Academy, the Study Skills Program, Computer Creatives and CyberSlate.

Ben Bronz Academy

The Ben Bronz Academy is a full-time, state-approved day school for learning disabled students in 2nd through 12th grade. The syllabus includes all normally required elementary and high school courses, a full range of remedial classes and some vocational offerings.

Most of the sixty or more students enrolled annually stay for two or three years, during which time they learn techniques that allow them to catch up academically and cope successfully when they return to public or private schools. Those who choose to graduate from Ben Bronz Academy receive a high school diploma.

Ben Bronz is unique. School districts from across Connecticut refer students with learning disabilities to the Academy because of its consistent record of sending the students back to them in two or three years much more capable of functioning in a regular public school.

Given that research shows that 85% of students enrolled in special-education reading programs show no change in test scores at the end of the year (Carnine, 1982), this is remarkable. This achievement was recognized by the state of Connecticut in 1987 when it bestowed on Ben Bronz Academy the award for the best special education program in the state.

The Study Skills Program

The Study Skills Program is an after-school tutorial session which helps local students overcome learning difficulties. They develop strategies for active learning that result in independent study habits. Instruction takes place in individual tutorials and small group study sessions after class and in the summer.

Computer Creatives

During the month of July each year, Computer Creatives provides remedial classes in reading, arithmetic and writing with several computer-based activities and small group instruction. A recreational program at a local park, including swimming, rounds out the computer camp day. The Computer Creatives program is an outgrowth of the software Ian Spence has developed and networked so that all of the Ben Bronz students can practice a variety of skills at home using the Internet.

CyberSlate

CyberSlate will be an Internet expansion of the computer software programs currently available on the Learning Incentive's local area computer network. It is being created to provide the same intensive, computer-monitored, step-by-step educational programs to teach and practice an entire range of academic skills. It begins with touch typing, reading and arithmetic and will be expanded to other areas of curriculum in the near future.

The system is currently used on a daily basis by all Ben Bronz students to practice academic skills to fluent levels of performance at the Academy or from their homes. This computer network and its resident software provide instant data recording and feedback to the student based on Precision Teaching principles and using a computer-generated version of the Standard Celeration Chart. Teachers monitor the data and, based on the information, institute program changes.

Results from the system clearly demonstrate its ability to provide effective practices for students with real-time, data-based, decision-making capabilities.

In partnership with Michael Maloney and Michael Summers, the creators of *Mighty Math* and *Math Tutor*, and with research and development grants from Canada's National Research Council, these and other programs will soon be available on the World Wide Web at CyberSlate.ca. This site should significantly increase our ability to assist students, both children and adults, who are at risk of school failure or need to improve their literacy skills.

The Founders

The Learning Incentive was established in 1982 by Ian Spence and his wife, Aileen Stan-Spence, both Yeshiva University doctoral graduates. Both were working in a social-service environment and felt the need of a career change. Ian contemplated working in the quickly emerging computer industry. Odgen Lindsley, the creator of Precision Teaching, and a long-time colleague of the Spences, suggested to Ian that they continue to work in an area where they had expertise. Ogden advised them to pay a visit to our fledgling Quinte Learning Center. During July of 1982, Aileen and Ian spent most of a week surveying our work, asking questions and trying to come to a decision. By the fall of that year, The Learning Incentive was born. It turned out to be a short step for each of the founders, although it did seem daunting at the time.

As a former master classroom teacher, and later a faculty member at Yeshiva and Fairfield Universities, Aileen is a specialist at teacher training. Her research centers on the effective use of classroom time. She has also developed and field tested two highly effective programs, The Ben Bronz Reading System and The MetaLearning Program, a thinking and language program for the elementary grades. Ian is good at anything he puts his mind to, so it came as no surprise to anyone that the center was soon doing well.

The founders are ably assisted by Dr. Wells Hively, as research director, and Dr. Susan Sharp as Education Director of the Academy.

The Philosophy of The Learning Incentive / Ben Bronz Academy

The Learning Incentive / Ben Bronz Academy operate on the philosophy that students are "in the business of learning". The founders and staff believe that such learning is best served if the educational decisions made by or for the students are based on their current demonstrated performances rather than some doctrinaire pedagogy. Students are entitled to immediate feedback about their performances. These include their classroom behavior where they are continuously given information to become more aware of the effects of their behavior on their ability to perform. They are given "positives" for behaviors which contribute to their learning and "negatives " for those behaviors which interfere with their learning. Real-time data become fundamental to all educational decisions and must be collected and managed with peak efficiency.

The sources from which curricula are drawn are eclectic but must survive the test of demonstrating success using frequency-based measures. A student is expected to read 200 words per minute orally. If some program component looks promising, it may be incorporated because it builds skills more efficiently. It will continue to be used, if and only if the daily data show student reading improvement as a result.

In a very real sense, this learning center and school operate as an applied educational research setting in which the curriculum, the training and teaching methods, the activities and schedules, the personnel selection, and the student testing methods are all continuously evaluated and systematically improved based on student performance.

Educational Program Components at Ben Bronz Academy

The components which have led to the consistent successes at Ben Bronz include all of those of the original QLC model (behavior analysis/behavior modification, learning outcomes and behavioral objectives, Direct Instruction, Precision Teaching, directed and independent practice). They have added a strand of programming called Mediated Learning based on the research of Reuvan Feuerstein (1980) and expanded by Aileen Stan-Spence. This program helps students become aware of the language and thought processes they use in developing problem-solving strategies. These practices are included in two courses at the academy - the MetaLearning Program in the early grades and the Instrumental Enrichment Program in the later grades.

The Role of Computers

A multitude of networked computers are scattered across classrooms, offices and other areas of the Ben Bronz Academy. These are used by students daily, with and without a teacher present, to practice skills. Each student also has a computer at home with data transferred to the center as the student works.

To promote the development of what have become to be known in Precision Teaching as "fluent performances" (Binder, 1996), Ian Spence has built a customized and sophisticated network of classroom computers. Through the computerization of the Standard Celeration Chart (Lindsley, 1971), he, the students and the staff are able to continuously monitor progress without the time-consuming step of keeping and organizing numerous charts which require data plotting by the teacher and/or the student.

Students are expected to work on developing their fluencies during the Fluency Practice periods as part of their "business of learning". These are scheduled for set times of the school day. Each consists of a series of one-minute practices in tool skills like typing, math facts, reading skills and vocabulary skills. Each student's programs are individualized. They work on various "pinpoints" as often as they get the opportunity during the school day or at home at night. Their best score for the day becomes the score to surpass the following day until fluency is achieved at that level and a new level commences.

The typing program develops keyboarding skills that are necessary for fluent use of other pinpoints. It has four major components: finger placement (25 levels), typing words (30+ levels), home stretch (25 levels) and typing sentences (20 levels). Students work on one or more of these 100+ levels each day for at least one attempt. They immediately see their progress charted and reported to them. They can quickly and easily compare their current performances to their past attempts, can see how many levels they have completed or where they may need help.

Results from Ben Bronz Academy

Ian and Aileen Spence report that students referred to the Academy are of average or above average intelligence, but are so learning disabled that their regular school has made a referral or the parents have elected to pay the tuition. Of 112 students surveyed over the past 6 years, 52 were roughly two or more grades below grade level as measured by standardized testing when they were enrolled (Hively, Stan-Spence, Spence, and Sharp, 1998a, 1998b). Like Quinte Learning Center and the other sites, students at Ben Bronz Academy have consistently gained 2 or more grade levels per year of study in reading, writing, spelling, and math as measured on standard tests such as the Gates-McGinitie and Woodcock-Johnson. The Spences and their staff have been able to consistently remediate the academic deficits of their students and have them return successfully to their school systems.

The Haughton Learning Center (Napa, California) - Elizabeth Haughton, Founder

Elizabeth Haughton founded the Haughton Learning Center in December of 1988 in a shopping mall in Napa, California. She later expanded it in the same site to serve a growing list of clients. Like her predecessors, she started with only herself and two or three children and slowly but steadily grew to have a staff of ten teachers and a bustling center of 60 plus students. Unlike all of the other centers, Elizabeth has refused the enticement to develop her business into a full-time day school. It remains a center for school supplement, not school replacement. Her goal, like those of the others who have adopted this general model, is to catch kids up at a faster than normal rate and to help them acquire the fluent skills they will require to be successes in school and in life.

The Haughton Learning Center is principally based on Precision Teaching practices more than any of the other technologies.

The Students

Each center attracts those individuals who are at risk of school failure or who are already failing. Elizabeth's students range from five years of age to adulthood, but are most often between the ages of seven and twelve. Almost all have a history of learning difficulties in their regular classrooms. Some have the designation of being labeled learning disabled. Others are followed by their siblings after the results begin to emerge.

The Program

The Haughton Learning Center has somewhat less reliance on prepackaged Direct Instruction programs. Almost exclusively, teaching is done on a one-to-one basis with intensive instruction and frequent practice timings. Tutorials usually last for one hour, typically twice, but sometimes as many as five times per week. Each student may have 10 - 15 different academic measures ongoing at any one time, all of which are charted for decision making. The Haughton Learning Center conducts monthly curriculum checks with the homeschool to see that the progress made at the center is affecting the student's everyday learning.

Academic and social skills management practices are behavioral in that along with praise, they include the use of a Learning Bank program. When students reach fluency aims in specific chunks of curriculum, they get to deposit their learning in the learning bank. When they make the 20th deposit in their learning account, they receive $20 from the Center. A deposit could be a set of five practice sheets on the same skill, such as reading a set of five poems at a fluent rate, or perhaps five different math sheets on a chunk of math curriculum.

Results

Because students from The Haughton Learning Center are not being withdrawn from a public or private school to be given an intensive remedial program and then returned, Elizabeth and her staff have less need of standardized educational testing. They don't have to prove to some principal or school administrator that the student has made sufficient progress to justify placement in an advanced grade. The staff at Haughton Learning Center has only the parents and students to satisfy that the program is working.

Some of Elizabeth's students have been involved in testing in their schools after they have been students at the center. Results of these students are consistent with those of the other centers, with children gaining two years in the subject areas tutored for each year in the program.

Innovations

Elizabeth and her staff are always on the hunt for new and better ways to improve a student's performance. She began to notice that students with reading and language difficulties were often not fluent in their auditory processing skills. They found it difficult to tell one sound from another or to sequence sounds. These students needed fluent levels of skills to discriminate between the sounds they would later be expected to read. They would also need much more competent blending skills to be able to use these sounds to decode words. Elizabeth and her staff are creating an Auditory Processing program to address the needs of these students as a prerequisite to reading. A version of this program is also in use at the Ben Bronz Academy.

The Cache Valley Learning Center (Logan, Utah) - Anne Desjardins, Founder

The Startup

The various centers that have sprung from our original work have adapted to a wide range of environments. From towns like Napa, California, to small cities of 40,000 like Belleville, Ontario, and Logan, Utah, to medium-sized cities in densely populated areas like West Hartford, Connecticut, to a metropolis like Seattle, Washington, they have taken root and flourished.

They survive nicely in provinces like Ontario, where educational funding eats up half of the municipal budget, to places like Utah, a state which consistently spends less on education than most states of the union.

The Cache Valley Learning Center is unique in that it is being developed in a culture which is much more homogeneous than that of any of the other sites. Against this Mormon backdrop, where family values continue to be a very high priority, and where no other private school exists within a hundred miles, Anne Desjardins and her staff have developed a successful center and school in record time.

Having been instrumental in the development of both Quinte Learning Center and Morningside Learning Center, Anne was well-prepared for the challenges of creating her own establishment. Beginning in the fall of 1992, Anne instituted the classic pattern of starting a tutorial center which grew to serve forty to fifty children in after-school remediation. The needs of the students and the push from the parents resulted in Anne forming a private school in 1995. Beginning with 15 students, the Cache Valley School has expanded to over 60 children from kindergarten through 8th grade in a full-day academic program. The after-school tutorials remain, and like the other centers, a summer school has been added. The full-day school program includes the arts, physical education, science and the other content subjects.

As the center grew to become a school, the staff expanded to seven full-time and three part-time teachers, including some with advanced degrees, three masters and one Ph.D.

Results

As with the other sites where students are expected to return to a public school system, Anne has buttressed her in-class data with the kinds of academic tests most schools use. The pattern of results is again replicated with children gaining at least two years of academic progress for each year spent at the school.

The more sophisticated data include the daily measures of specific skills from the point of instruction until they have become fluent. These are the data upon which decisions are based that ultimately generate the rapid skill development and the jump in grade levels indicated on the standardized tests.

Crystal Del Zompo - A Student's Personal Success Story

Crystal Del Zompo's story is similar to that of literally thousands of children who have passed through the doors of all these centers over the past two decades. Her story appeared

177

in the March, 1997, edition of *Learning Success*, a newsletter published by the Haughton Learning Center.

Despite previously having had several tutors, including a reading specialist, Crystal still could not read at the end of third grade. She would not attempt to write even simple sentences. Mary Del Zompo, Crystal's mother, noted that her daughter was becoming withdrawn and avoided direct eye contact. She "had low self-esteem and didn't want to go to school."

Once she became a student at Haughton Learning Center, according to Mary, "Her whole demeanor changed rapidly." Crystal's skills in reading, spelling and writing have improved so dramatically that she now writes complete stories. She is no longer afraid to make class presentations. She has not only become a competent student, but has even made the Honor Roll at Silverado Middle School.

Crystal's experience has taught her that she would like to work in a center like Elizabeth's and help children such as herself who have difficulty in school. Mary Del Zompo is convinced that having Crystal in Elizabeth's hands has changed her life forever. "The difference has been like night and day", she says. "Haughton Learning Center has helped Crystal feel good about herself and her learning."

Summary

It is clear from the data of the various learning centers we have created, and from those with whom we have shared our technologies, that these integrated methods work equally well in a variety of settings, managed by different individuals, with a diversity of clients and programs. This, combined with the Follow Through and Sacajawea data and that from other behavioral programs, makes a very convincing empirical argument, especially given the current public school achievement record, for effective school reform.

Literally thousands of clients, both children and adults, have had their learning difficulties successfully remediated in these centers in the past 20 years. The work continues and is slowly being expanded. We have built the better mouse trap - in classrooms, on factory floors, in software, in cyberspace and in some schools where political intervention seemed the only answer. Why has public education not beaten a path to our door? We have existed for almost two decades; we have published our research and we have invited all comers. Nonetheless, we have yet to make an impact on public schools.

Part Six

• •

Leading the
Horse to Water

If It's So Good, Why Don't Schools Use It?

● ●

"If you build a better mouse trap,
the world will beat a path to your door."
- Emerson

The obvious question arises: if any one or more of these technologies is so effective, why don't the schools use them? If it can be empirically demonstrated that one of these technologies or better still, some combination of them is even more powerful in its impact on illiteracy, why have they not been widely adopted in North American schools?

Like many complex questions, it could have a simple answer, but simple answers to complex questions are generally wrong. The answer is much more complicated and is influenced by a number of factors. We will examine them individually in this chapter.

It Isn't Taught to Teachers

The simplest reason that these technologies are not used in schools is that they are not taught to teachers when they are trained. Courses on effective methods are rarely part of the syllabus of teacher-training institutions. There are almost no courses in Behavior Analysis and Behavior Modification, Direct Instruction or Precision Teaching among the offerings of most teacher education centers in North America. It is little wonder the teachers are ignorant of these methods. The people who prepare them for the classroom simply don't make them skilled in or even aware of these systems.

183

A Good Index of Awareness

A classic example of this lack of awareness occurred when I was invited to give a lecture at Queen's University in Kingston, Ontario, where the Ministry of Education and Training hosts teachers' courses each summer. The students were in the final semester of the Special Education Specialist program. Since these courses required teachers to take three annual segments in order to achieve their special education designation, I was addressing professionals who had a minimum of two years' teaching experience beyond their teacher training. Most had many more years under their belts than that. I began each lecture by asking if anyone was aware of the Head Start program. A few people in each class had some vague idea of it as an American educational initiative, but no one had any specific knowledge. I then asked if anyone knew about Project Follow Through. In the three years I made this presentation to approximately 200 teachers, not one of them was able to tell me about the largest, most expensive, longest-running, comparative study of special educational methods ever done in the Western world - one which involved thousands of "at-risk" students like the ones they were seeking to help. If they were unaware of a study of this magnitude, what else weren't they taught on their way to becoming specialists? Their response was to chastise me for not using Canadian research. Somehow they felt that American educational research didn't apply north of the border.

This says little for the teachers. It says far less for their professors and for the courses which they are presenting to turn out educational specialists. It does point out rather dramatically the degree to which empirical data and published research fails to impact teacher training. While this is admittedly a limited sample, the same lack of attention to research is a common experience of other trainers with whom I have worked.

Schools and Data

Another of the major reasons why these technologies are

184

not more widely implemented is a function of the ways in which schools make decisions. Principals, school authorities and elected school officials are not particularly well-known for their empirical approach to solving academic problems. They are largely unaware of the data. They don't know the research and they don't let the data get in the way of their decisions.

Teachers, too, generally do not read research reports. The journals are not commonly available in most school libraries or staff rooms. Discussions of the latest educational breakthroughs were rarely topics on the agenda of any staff meeting I ever attended as a teacher. There were few, if any, systematic attempts to introduce new methods. Oftentimes, problems like lateness, fighting and skipping school which these technologies have been highly successful at solving, were recurring agenda items, but no systematic review of the research literature to determine a better solution ever made the list for discussion.

Where Have Half of the Smart Teachers Gone?

One research study by the Rand Corporation (1982) may give some insight into teachers' ignorance of empirical research. The study attempted to elucidate the reasons for the perceived decline in the quality of graduates from American universities across a number of disciplines. Knowing that there is a core set of questions that appear on every Scholastic Aptitude Test, Rand researchers decided to compare the scores of applicants on these particular questions across generations. They found that the scores did drop for all candidates across a number of seven-year periods. And they dropped for each discipline - medicine, engineering, business and the arts. But the most precipitous decline occurred with those students choosing education as their major area of study.

These same researchers then decided to follow up on these candidates five years later to see what had happened to them professionally. With the teachers, they discovered that fully 50% of them were no longer in the teaching profession. Those who left the profession were the 50% with the highest scores of the educators on the S.A.T. Given that many students who select a liberal arts college program do not have a strong background in math and science, and given that many of the higher scoring candidates leave the profession within five years, it is not surprising that those remaining are not found pouring over the statistics of the latest educational research publications.

The Facts, Nothing but the Facts

Schools generally have not used hard data as a part of student, teacher or program evaluation. If it happens at all, the data will most likely be a pre- and post-measure using a standardized test. While this is better than nothing, it is nowhere near that which is easily possible with Precision Teaching practices. This option is not appealing to teachers or to school administrators because sometimes the data point out deficits that they would rather not see and for which they have no programs, staffing, materials or training.

The lack of data in schools, except for anecdotal reports, which is as close as most schools come to data gathering, is a direct result of the philosophical position most schools have adopted in the last half-century.

The Child-Centered Approach to Learning

One of the major determinants on how teachers think and act is a result of the philosophy of the teacher trainers who taught them. North American Education is greatly influenced by the child-centered approach that began at Columbia University's Teacher College in the 1920s and 1930s. It is still predominant today, despite its notable lack of success, and despite the heritage of literacy and numeracy problems it has bequeathed to us.

In his book, *The Schools We Need and Why We Don't Have Them*, E.D. Hirsch points out that if it was possible for thousands of Soviet planners and economists to be wrong about an economic model like communism, it would be equally plausible that a group of educational theorists could be wrong about an educational philosophy in North America.

He says, "If thousands of Marxist thinkers could have been caught for decades in the grip of a wrong socio-economic theory, it is not beyond imagination that a cadre of American educational experts could have been captivated by wrong theories over roughly the same period."

It appears that they were and continue to be wrong-headed and yet they still hold sway in almost every teacher training institution on the continent. They fend off criticism in unique ways.

Their strategy is a little like the verbal equivalent to Brer Fox and the Tar Baby. The more Brer Fox hit and kicked at the tar baby, the more he became frustrated and covered in its tar. The more empiricists attack the lack of specificity in the child-centered approach, the more they are painted as anti-child and anti-independent learning.

The "Progressive" Approach . . .

The child-centered philosophy, in its most basic form, believes in an "ages and stages" approach to cognitive development. It assumes that the child will learn when he is "ready". Hirsch discusses the use of terminology by "progressive" educators to fend off any incursion of those who favor accountability. The emphasis by "progressive" educators is on the use of words like "child-centered", and "developmentally appropriate", which sound good but are left almost totally undefined. The great advantage to "progressive" educators in their use of generalized, non-measurable concepts and applications is in the very fact that they cannot be measured against any concrete standard and, therefore, cannot be held accountable. Such measurement is considered by them as "traditional" and "inappropriate". Progressive teachers want to see the individual development of each child in their classes, not the comparison of some tested performance against a district, state or national average.

What develops is a war of words in which child-centered

theorists dismiss any practice of empirical educators as boring and totally out of touch with the times. At the same time, they create the notion that learning is fun, relevant and interesting if taught by a "progressive" teacher. This is an easy sell to parents who want their children to enjoy school and not be placed in what could appear to be an academic pressure cooker with their progress compared to others. Parents at all levels typically will not insist on specific objective measures of progress, and in so doing, give up their chance to hold the system accountable.

. . . Versus Tried and True

The technologies outlined in the Quinte Learning Center model are anathema to child-centered educators. The components utilized in this model would not only never be used by them, they would be roundly criticized, despite their consistently exemplary results. They would be seen as slavish, uncreative, repetitious regimens into which groups of students are herded like sheep. Attacks from these quarters are not infrequent and are sometimes more politically than scientifically motivated.

The House, McLean, Glass censure of the Follow Through results is a good example of such criticism. Funded by the Ford Foundation (which also sponsored the Bank Street School, a child-centered model in the Follow Through project), House et al reanalyzed the data. To nobody's surprise, the Bank Street model came out on top. This research was presented at the 1982 International Reading Conference in Toronto. Both Engelmann and Becker, the Direct Instruction Model founders, were in the audience to hear their colleague, Carl Bereiter, rebut these results in a more systematic, site-by-site analysis which cast huge doubt on the "Glass House" study.

The Current Lack of Measurable Educational Standards

Given the almost wholesale adherence to child-centered

learning approaches by North American schools, it becomes difficult to expand the use of our particular technologies on the basis of the fact that they produce better results. The argument that they will increase test scores, reduce the percentage of illiterates, decrease school failure or impact drop-out rates is pretty much lost on educators in systems which have no demonstrable standards, except whether or not the students are "creative", "well-adjusted" or "interested in learning".

The idea of maintaining any consistent set of standards took another major hit with the adoption of the policy of "social promotion". Social promotion occurs when a student is moved to the next grade, despite a known lack of skills and/or performance, so that he will be with his age peers. The rationale is that to hold students back in the same grade is psychologically, socially or emotionally traumatic for them. No one wants to see a ten-year-old struggling to meet Grade Two standards with a group of seven and eight-year-olds. It is more humane to allow him into the next grade, regardless of his obvious inability to handle the current, let alone the subsequent curriculum. Usually, despite whatever plans are put in place to catch the child up and re-integrate him academically, the student falls further and further behind. In the last twenty years, we have dealt with literally hundreds of such students and have been able to remediate their deficient skills. Given that there are now a number of viable, demonstrated and effective alternatives which singly or in combination are an educational remedy, the call becomes easy. Teach the children well.

In fairness to most teachers, the option of social promotion occurs when they have done their level best with the tools they possess, in the time the student was available to them. They may very well be completely unaware of the options presented by the technologies we endorse. Until they can see that this is not just another educational fad, it's fair for them to use what they know best. It is our responsibility to present the evidence and make available the information which will allow them to make a different decision.

Grade Equivalent Diplomas

Standards are further eroded by the granting of grade-equivalent diplomas. These are diplomas that are earned by passing an exam as opposed to amassing a required number of credits. The same standards that are demanded in credit courses could be built into a grade-equivalent diploma and then there could be a point-to-point correspondence between the two diplomas. But that does not currently happen. It doesn't even happen with the diplomas granted by different schools or systems in the absence of a common final examination set and marked by the state or provincial jurisdiction. As a result, it is relatively easier to pass a grade-equivalent diploma exam than it is to pass the necessary courses for an actual diploma.

The grade-equivalent diploma often winds up giving the student the appearance of being a high-school graduate without the skills. The backlash from employers is to discount all secondary-school diplomas as not being any type of qualifier for job applicants. The employers soon learn to distrust the system that generates these graduates and resent the tax payments which fund them.

In Ontario, the Ministry of Education and Training allows a student to earn "life-experience" credits if they leave school early without a diploma and then return. Individuals may earn up to two credits per year for each year they have been out of school, up to a total of nine credits. These credits are not awarded on the basis of any particular life experiences. Just being able to breathe is enough. To graduate with an Ontario Secondary School Diploma, the student needs a total of thirty credits, almost a third of which they can acquire by staying alive. Such a practice hardly encourages faith in any academic standards set by the Ministry.

Given the elastic nature of current standards, it is not surprising that teachers, principals and system administrators are not diligently seeking out and using the best available teaching methods in order to meet the marks set by their system. The standards don't exist so there simply is no need to do so. The situation is likely to remain in this state until school systems set and operate on the basis of measurable standards which are well and easily understood by teachers, students, parents, and employers.

Lack of Contingencies for Ineffective Teaching

At the present time, there are no contingencies for teachers who do not do an adequate job of teaching. If a number of children in a classroom do not show evidence of learning, there is usually no penalty for the teacher. Sometimes teachers, who are known to be inept, will be transferred to a distant school or to a more difficult assignment with the hope that they will leave the profession. Sometimes they do; more often they do not.

With the lack of hard comparative data, it becomes much more difficult to ferret out the incompetent teacher. When this does happen, it is usually the result of persistent complaints by a succession of parents until it gets to the point where it can no longer be ignored by the principal and the superintendent. The problem of getting rid of an incompetent teacher has become an arduous task with the rise of powerful teacher organizations.

As boards of education have consolidated across North America in the past thirty years, the teachers have become better organized into unions and professional organizations. They are now a political force to be dealt with in many jurisdictions. The present Premier of Ontario, Mike Harris, found this out in spades in October of 1997, when his controversial legislation for school reform (Bill C-160) led to the largest teachers' strike in the history of North American education.

Unfortunately, the teachers' associations do not police their members or cull out the ineffective individuals within their ranks with any more ardor than other professions like law or medicine. Each profession has its bad apples and its incompetents. Unfortunately, teachers' unions use their growing power to protect even the most inept of their associates. Teachers' unions like those in Ontario, whose pension funds contain more wealth than the entire Canadian Pension Plan, have very much become a force most local boards do not go out of their way to do battle with. As a result, like many professions, teachers have become very comfortable that the level of accountability will never grow to the point where lack of performance might threaten their job.

Given that they have no fear of retribution for not doing an adequate job, there is no impetus by mediocre or poor teachers to improve their teaching skills. They will hardly go hunting for a program that will cause them more work, even if it gets the results. The teachers who do adopt these technologies are most often those who are already the most diligent and dedicated and always on the lookout for better means to teach.

The Pain of Change

Another reason that these technologies have never been widely adopted is that they require a tremendous amount of change from normal patterns of behavior. It takes better skills and preparation to develop and manage a behavior modification program than it does to assign a detention or send the student to the principal's office.

It takes much better organization of the classroom to run a Direct Instruction program with two or three groups of children than it does to present a whole-class reading lesson.

It adds work to the teacher's day to manage even a couple of charts per child in a Precision Teaching approach to measurement. And all of the additional practice, especially the written work, does not correct itself. It all requires time and effort.

Any one of these technologies will produce gains, but only at the cost of committing to increased teaching and more time spent on management, additional measurement and practice time. There are a number of ways in which structural and procedural changes can be made to alleviate some of these pressures, but in the final analysis, a dedicated teacher using these technologies will work harder than a colleague who uses standard-brand teaching methods. As long as it is perfectly acceptable to use existing programs, despite their often dismal results, there is no incentive for even the best teachers to adopt new methods. Change entails disruption and pain. The status quo is so much more comfortable.

There is a proportion of teachers who will try just about anything if they think it will benefit their students. They are the top guns of the teaching profession. There are larger numbers who are willing to attempt something new if they can be shown its efficacy and be provided with the appropriate training and resources. This constitutes the bulk of teachers - competent, hard-working, intelligent, and dedicated to producing good students. There are a few others who can be cajoled or ordered to make changes. They will do so only under duress and without any real commitment or enthusiasm, complaining all the while. Almost every school staff has at least one of these - someone waiting for a pension. There are also a few teachers who simply refuse to implement new programs under almost any circumstances. They close their classroom doors and go on doing what they have always done, secure in the knowledge that the new program will go away like those before it and that the principal is not very likely to come and sit in their classrooms to monitor the situation.

The principal who attempts to be a change agent in introducing these behavioral technologies faces a daunting task in most schools. He causes significant disruption to the staff with the proposed changes, adds to budget costs, creates needs for training, and, other than expected student gains, is unlikely to be rewarded for taking the lead. It's easier to stand pat.

Being Too Successful

Adopting these technologies is a double-edged sword. On one edge is the pain of change, on the other, the pain of success. When a teacher becomes the best behavior manager in the school, he attracts undisciplined kids like a magnet to his classroom. When the teacher begins to produce the results in reading or math that consistently flow from well-managed Direct Instruction programs, he is often rewarded with more deficient readers to teach. When the teacher engages in daily measurement of critical learning skills and changes the rate at which students learn, he may become the recipient of those students who need the most help. The successful teacher is "rewarded" with more and more difficult tasks for having been a success. The process generally continues until the teacher burns out and abandons the programs from sheer exhaustion and lack of support.

Successful implementation of these technologies generally cannot be done by a single teacher or even a small segment of the staff unless some safeguards are provided to prevent inundating them with the mountain of academic needs that each school faces. A limited program with one or two teachers and a defined number of students can add enormously to any school's ability to impact literacy problems. As staff begins to see the benefits, and with leadership focused on measurable results and meeting high standards, a school can radically change its capacity to produce skillful, knowledgeable students, regardless of their previous learning histories or diagnoses.

Why Can't MY Child Be in that Class?

Once these technologies become part of a school, and the success becomes evident, parents begin to hear about "the new program". In most schools, there is not a wholesale adoption of these technologies. They tend to be instituted by one individual, or at best a couple of teachers. When that teacher begins to make readers out of children who had previously not been taught to read, it does reverberate throughout the parent community of the school. When they ask to have their child included and are told that the class is full, the next problem occurs. They want to know why their child's teacher isn't doing the same thing, using the same program. The successful teacher is sometimes envied, sometimes ostracized, and sometimes even sabotaged.

If teacher participation in such programs is voluntary, and the teachers who adopt the programs get better results, there is pressure for other teachers to change. If these teachers are resistant, there is a greatly increased tension among the staff.

Staff morale is a major concern of principals, many of whom take the position that is better not to use the programs than to have unhappy teachers.

Remediating Other Teacher's Failures

Another significant problem arises when the child who was not expected to do well academically begins to blossom under the influence of better academic programming. The teachers who failed to teach that student because of his "learning problem" are unmasked for what they are - inadequate instructors. There is no more dramatic example of this than the student who has been diagnosed with "dyslexia" and has a file an inch thick with reports of failed attempts over a period of years. Suddenly, this student becomes a reader in a matter of months in a Direct Instruction Corrective Reading Program. The question of what happened to his "dyslexia" becomes of interest and the diagnosis is seen for what it is - "dysteachia".

If one listens to the professional psychologists who test kids and label them, but who have probably never actually taught one to read and would have few clues about where to begin, "dyslexia" is a real entity, not a reversible condition resulting from incompetent instruction. Parents and teachers are told that "dyslexia" is a continuum of reading difficulty ranging from mild to moderate, to severe and profound. Parents and teachers really should be told that dyslexia is produced by inept teachers or nonfunctional reading programs that create "dysteachia", a continuum of instructional deficits that ranges from mild to moderate, to severe and profound. Almost without exception, dyslexia can be reversed by a competent teacher with a Direct Instruction reading program and some daily reading measurements.

Good Teachers are Born, Not Made

Teachers who turn other teachers' failures into functioning students are treated in one of two ways. They are either labeled "gifted" or they are ostracized. The "gifted" label gets every other merely mortal teacher off the hook. *They* could never be expected to deliver the level of teaching of "The Great One", any more than they could play hockey on a line with Wayne Gretzsky. The effect is that competent teaching is interpreted as an accident of heredity, not a set of skills that any concerned teacher could easily learn.

It supports the notion that good teachers are born, not made. If we really believed that, we would abandon the teacher-training programs and replace them with some type of litmus test for genetically predisposed teachers. But to the non-critical parent, the explanation that this "special" teacher has extraordinary skills is often sufficient to have them not ask about why other teachers can't do this. And while it is true that some teachers are more gifted than some of their peers, they will often admit it is mostly due to plain hard work, a fine mentor, a great program or some combination. They don't feel "special". For twenty years I have trained teachers whom parents have raved about. All those I have trained are well aware that it is the training, the technology, the diligence and the philosophy that *every* child can learn that makes the difference.

Handing Over Competent Kids to Mediocre Teachers

There are times when an innovative approach is used successfully by a teacher or team of teachers. They work diligently to make a difference and then hand the students over to a teacher who is not committed to excellence and they watch helplessly as the students slide downhill again. There are few more discouraging scenarios for a committed teacher than to know that their students have been sentenced to at least a year with a dullard and their good efforts will not be carried on.

Elucidating the Deficits - A Frightening Pattern Emerges

With the use of good academic measures like those available to Precision Teaching, there is an added threat. The measurement system is simple and sensitive. It quickly identifies the progress of any student on any particular skill. It can measure that skill several different ways in a matter of minutes, without having a psychometrist or psychologist in the building.

A measurement program can be established to have each student do several common pinpoints in reading, spelling, math, etc. At the end of each week or month, the data can be collated to show the overall progress of the students by grade, by subject, or both. The data soon highlights children who are doing well and those who are not progressing. When a pattern begins to emerge where some or all of the students in a particular class are not making gains, it sends up red flags about a situation that may need inspection. This kind of accountability scares the hell out of some teachers. It becomes very obvious whose students are making achievements and whose are not.

If these data become public information at parent or school board meetings, the resulting furor can be pretty uncomfortable for teachers, principals and school officials. Again, it is easier not to get involved in such a process, and regrettably, that's what most schools do.

Rationalizing the System's Failure

In the thirty years that I have spent in education, I have heard only one teacher admit that the reason the child was not succeeding was that he had failed to teach him well. Most of the time the system finds a way to deflect any hint of responsibility for the failures it creates. It points to its successes and takes full credit for them. The inference inherent in this message is that, "If these kids can do it and yours can't, it must be your kid, 'cause look here, we have all of these others who are able."

With the lack of any objective standards it is difficult to make the case that a particular student is weak in this or that area of study. When parents feel that there is a difficulty, it is often hard to get the data to demonstrate their concern. They also run head-on into a raft of explanations about why their child may be behind. Many times standardized test results are used to convey to the parents the notion that their child is "different", and there is just not a whole lot the school can do about it. The problem is somehow the child, or maybe it's the parents themselves. There is a host of standard reasons for not fixing the problem. There is never enough staff, never enough money, never enough time to get to their child. Many parents accept this and go away, feeling that the school is doing its best and they will just have to live with it. Other parents become more insistent; they meet with the principal, the director, the specialists, the superintendent and generally they get the help they are seeking, although many times the extra "help" doesn't achieve much.

Teflon Schools

Schools also use concepts from the social sciences to explain why some children fail. Failure gets blamed on birth order, family history, genetic tendencies and perceptual problems which again are inside the child's head and unable to be changed by instruction. Letter reversals, which are interpreted as "seeing things backwards", is a pretty common one, even though the same kid can hit a baseball, stickhandle a puck, tie his shoes and do many other visually-related tasks without difficulty. Strangely enough, with a little practice of the symbols being reversed, it also goes away.

The schools rely on a mantle of professionalism in order to appear expert in these matters. Their position allows them to fend off criticism or blame for failure like a Teflon-coated cooking pan. Unfortunately, most parents are too respectful or feel too much like novices to challenge the authorities with much persistence.

Given that schools can justify their failures in myriad ways, it relieves them of the necessity to change the rate of poor academic production or even of sustained failures.

Parents as Educational Consumers

Parents are not critical consumers of education. Most

frankly don't know what to expect from their school. They often don't know what to ask for, how to ask for it or even how to recognize it if it is given. Schools do not go out of their way, in many cases, to clarify the situation. It's as if schools are content not to have enlightened consumers because they may become more demanding if they are.

Parents are also reluctant to seriously challenge the school for fear that it will somehow affect the treatment of their child or children. Again, this provides a covering for the lack of performance which may go unchallenged.

Finally, parents have a certain degree of schizophrenia about their educational system. They generally like their child's teacher, they are okay with the school; they're maybe not as sure about the principal; they generally don't trust the superintendent, and the system in their view needs a lot of change. The further removed they are from the classroom teacher, the more distrustful they are about the system. That often leads to avoidance, a degree of impotence, and a sense of being disassociated from the system. It may help to explain why only 2% of parents ever attend a school board meeting despite the importance of education to them. Such parental attitudes and the resultant lack of action also foster no change and lessen the probability of systems adopting better technology or becoming more accountable.

Lack of Compensation for Teacher Achievement

There are no rewards for the teacher who makes a critical difference in his students' lives. The path to promotion does not necessarily result from excellent teaching. There are no extra paychecks, holidays, conferences or other perks for the competent teacher. Generally there is only more work. The only reward, and it is sufficient for a number of teachers, is the satisfaction of doing one's best and seeing the difference that it makes in the lives of people who would otherwise have been casualties.

In a society where information is power, and where knowledge is a capital asset, a good teacher is worth at least as much as a good doctor. But in a society where more money is spent on cosmetics than on education, that appreciation is not likely near at hand. Not feeling valued can develop into an excuse for not doing one's best. Like anyone else, teachers can become discouraged and lethargic if they are made to feel unworthy. It is hardly the motivation that will send them seeking newer or better answers.

Inept Marketing of Good Technologies

Yet another reason these technologies remain underused in the face of an international literacy crisis, is that their publishers have not been overly successful in marketing these programs to teachers and school boards, reading and math specialists, special educators or literacy agencies.

Much of the research and many of the methods for behavior analysis and behavior modification are published in poorly circulated journals and periodicals that most teachers would never see.

The Direct Instruction programs are marketed by Science Research Associates, a major educational publisher based in Chicago. They have, at times, held training sessions to familiarize teachers with the programs, but these have been sporadic and not hugely successful. Until recently, there was not even a well-marked Direct Instruction segment in their annual school catalogue.

Also, it is not SRA's responsibility to determine which programs should be used. Their job is to collect, publish and sell materials for classrooms to school districts. It is the school's mandate to find the very best products.

Precision Teaching materials have been handled by a small Kansas company, Behavior Research Co., owned by Ogden Lindsley, the creator of the technology. This firm has not had the wherewithal to launch a national sales and marketing effort of any significance. Recently, Precision Teaching materials have also been marketed and sold by Sopris West, a growing educational publishing house in Longmont, Colorado. Sopris West has just published a reworked version of many of the student materials from the original Sacajawea project. While it is a growing company, Sopris West is not yet a major national force in school publishing. As a result, its efforts in bringing Precision Teaching into the mainstream of elementary education is still limited.

The professional organizations - the Association for Behavior Analysis, the Association for Direct Instruction and the Standard Celeration Society - have not been terribly successful at increasing their new members or even keeping the members they have attracted. Their public relations and lobbying efforts have been, at best, sporadic and uncoordinated. Most teachers in classrooms in North America have never been directly approached by these organizations in the same way that other groups, like the Council for Exceptional Children, have done by developing local and regional branches. That may explain why C.E.C.'s membership is larger than the combined membership of the three aforementioned organizations involved with these technologies.

Failure to Achieve Acceptable Levels of Technology Transfer

Of the creators of effective behavioral technologies, Engelmann has been, by far, the most adept at transferring his technology to the marketplace. *Math Tutor*, QLC's software, had some degree of success in the North American school market for a decade with Scholastic. The learning center founders are beginning to transfer behavioral teaching systems to more and more places, but generally speaking, we have failed to achieve acceptable levels of technology transfer in education.

Other behavioral areas have had more impact. The field of behavioral safety has had some successes, notably in the work of Beth Sulzer-Azaroff, Aubrey Daniels, Scott Geller and Terry McSween. They have made inroads into the health and safety practices of corporate America. Beth Sulzer-Azaroff's book, *Who killed my daddy? A behavioral safety fable.* is a landmark publication in that field. An annual Behavioral Safety conference is now coordinated by the Cambridge Center for Behavioral Studies to further this work.

201

Hank Pennypacker, the founder of Mammacare Inc., has successfully impacted the field of medicine, specifically oncology, with his breast self-examination training products. Pennypacker and Hench (1997) recently wrote an article attempting to explain the lack of success in transferring behavioral research to marketable products and practices. They cite the lack of any overall strategies as the cause of this failure.

Certainly this is not the case with Direct Instruction. The failure of this exemplary instructional system to be a major influence is due much more to the lack of emphasis by schools on what works than by any lack of strategy to get the product to market. Schools reject Direct Instruction because they can do so with impunity. There is no penalty for the academic child abuse that results from not using the best tools available.

This lack of consequences for not using effective tools is in desperate need of change. School systems must be held accountable more for the academic gains they are funded to produce than for managing the brick and mortar, buses and teacher contracts that get most of their attention.

Summary

The various elements of the QLC model, singly or in combination, have so far, in twenty-five years, failed to make significant inroads into North American classrooms. Where they have been used, they have most often been abandoned, despite their effectiveness. The lack of standards in schools, the lack of accountability, and the pressures of good results to force other teachers to change all figure into the equation as to why these technologies remain on the shelf while thousands of children are sacrificed to illiteracy each year. The inability of the publishers to sell the advantages of these programs to teachers and the lack of schools' perception of their need to change are also factors. If we want to see changes in the students as the result of the implementation of better methods, we are going to have to address the issue of how to change schools.

Creating
Educational Change

• •

"He that will not apply new remedies
must expect new evils."
- Bacon

Major Questions

Irrespective of the origin of educational change forces, a number of major questions must be considered in revamping education:

- Who represents whom?
- How is representation decided and what powers do officials have?
- Who pays the bills and how is that decided?
- How do we allocate the resources in a fair and consistent manner?
- Who determines the standards and how are they measured?
- Who should be held accountable?
- Is there an adequate system in place to determine and ensure accountability?
- How do we attend to special needs of children and communities?

There have been discussions and arguments over these questions as long as there have been schools. The history of educational change in North America is replete with attempts to answer these and other queries.

A Concise History of Educational Change

It could appear to the casual observer that the educational reform movement is a new entity. This is not true. The history of both Canada and the United States shows a continuous pattern of various reforms since the establishment of the first schools.

In both countries, schools were initially founded by the town or township of which they were a part. These early school boards were supported directly by a property tax levy, with locally elected trustees having responsibility for management issues such as hiring, firing, and administrating the school. This meant that it was a community-based operation. Provincial or state education departments generally provided inspectors and some legislation regarding the establishment and funding of the schools. In most provinces and states, provision was also made for schools of various religious denominations, so that two school boards often operated in the same district, one public and one parochial. The community used the school for a wide variety of activities - as a meeting place, for polling stations, emergency shelters and various other functions. Generally, the residents felt some kind of bond to their community school.

The Need for Public Education

In the past, there was great controversy about whether universal elementary-level schooling was even necessary and whether or not it should be paid for through public taxation. The same debate regarding property taxes as a source for funding elementary and secondary education still rages today .

In those early days, some reformers saw public education as a way to end the abuses of child labor; others opposed it because they saw it as a means for the dominant class to train and enslave a work force for the factories of the emerging industrial revolution.

From the 1850s, North America experienced a wave of European immigration, dramatically increasing the size of its cities. The resultant slums and use of child labor led to an outcry for universal public education at least to the beginning high-school level. Some leaders, like Thomas Jefferson, saw public schools as a way to guarantee an enlightened electorate which would preserve a nascent democracy. He was successful in getting legislation passed in Virginia for tax-supported elementary and secondary schools with free tuition for bright, underprivileged children. A comprehensive review of this history was published by Rippa in 1992.

The Beginnings of Amalgamation

As a result of the continuing urbanization resulting from the Industrial Revolution during the late 1800s, some school boards began to amalgamate and administer several schools.

Even in the 1890s, groups began to articulate their dissatisfaction with the way schools were run, considering them far too autocratic and teacher-directed. They were at odds with those who saw students as empty vessels to be filled, not interactive organisms to explore and inquire. This discontent resulted in the formulation of many of the child-centered theories that became popular over the next twenty years and still dominate education today.

The first efforts to develop a common curriculum for elementary schools evolved during this period. McGinitie Readers and the idea of grades from one to eight evolved, partly because of the fact that these Readers were in a series of eight.

Schools did not experience dramatic changes until the end of the Second World War.

After World War II

At the end of WW II, more widespread structural changes were made in North American education. As the costs of education continued to increase, provincial and state legislatures began to subsidize school boards with insufficient tax bases due to small populations or ones with low-income residents. They wanted to ensure some degree of equity for school boards and the services they were expected to provide. In both countries, education was seen to be a state or provincial matter, with little federal involvement.

As the school districts continued to amalgamate in the late 50s and early 60s, the entire educational process began to become distanced from local control and more and more bureaucratized and professionalized. In the amalgamations of the 50s, the number of school boards in the U.S. dropped by 50% to 40,000. By 1970, there were only about 18,000 U.S. school boards. Today, according to Quality Education Research (1997), there are 16,386 school districts. Of the largest, 223 account for 30% of the nation's educational spending.

The same trend has occurred in Canada, with the most recent change in Ontario reducing its 129 school boards to 72 as a result of provincial legislation. By the same legislation, the Ontario government also removed educational funding from the municipal tax arena. They took over direct provincial funding of schools, swapping it for the cost of other social services, like welfare. New Brunswick, Alberta and recently, Newfoundland, are also making significant reductions in their school district numbers.

The end of the Second World War also marked the beginning of the baby boom. This caused a dramatic increase in the need for schools, teachers and educational spending in the late 50s and throughout the 60s. As schools scrambled to keep up, state and provincial governments began to play a larger and larger role in all facets of education, from capital funding of schools to teacher training and curriculum development. School bureaucracies burgeoned, budgets doubled and tripled. Teachers organized into unions and demanded more money, more benefits, professional development time and other concessions which they generally won in one district and then used as a basis for negotiation with other districts.

As the professionalization of teaching occurred, the relationships between school and community became even more distanced and more formalized, making parents sometimes feel like strangers in their own local schools.

The original stakeholders, the parents, the taxpayers, the trustees and even the students, became further disenfranchised and, in many cases, alienated from the educational process.

"Professional educators" took over the reins of power, and turned many boards into docile committees who rarely seriously challenged the administration, but simply rubber-stamped its decisions.

The takeover of some aspects of school funding by municipal, state, provincial and even the federal government also removed much of the financial onus for schools from the immediate community. This created a rift between taxpayers with children in the schools and others who paid taxes that supported schools even though they had no children enrolled. The issue of community versus parental responsibility for education further eroded the sense of community as the mill rate climbed and the tax bills rose. This issue remains unresolved and is a critical economic factor in school reform. Who is going to pay for it?

The Age of Expansion

Andrew Nikiforuk describes in his book, *School's Out*, the expansion of schools during the fifties, sixties and seventies. He reports that Canada spent 1.8% of the Gross National Product on schooling in the fifties. This grew to 3.2% by 1960 and to 7.2% in the late 1990s. This results in an expenditure of 32 billion dollars for 300,000 teachers to provide basic educational services.

The incredible rate of spending that began with the baby boom has simply never abated, despite declining enrollment in the 70s and 80s. Much of these additional funds was allocated to non-teaching personnel who came to represent 30% to 40% of all educational positions. Ontario and New York State, with populations between twenty and thirty million, each had as many educational administrators for their systems as did *all* of Western Europe with a population of three hundred million!

The effect of these additional costs has meant the re-allocation of funds, with a greater and greater proportion being gobbled up in administrative costs, and less and less reaching the classroom. Although the per pupil funding has doubled in the past three decades, and the teacher/pupil ratio has been reduced (at least on paper), teachers still face shortages of textbooks, support materials and even pencils and paper.

The Sputnik Effect

When the Russians launched Sputnik, the first space satellite in 1957, at the height of the Cold War with the "Evil Republic", the impact on North American education was stunning and immediate. The fear that North Americans were falling behind in science and math led to the passage of The National Defense Act. The American federal government spent millions of dollars on the "improvement" of the teaching of these subjects. Organizations like the National Science Foundation joined forces with the federal government to revamp the teaching of science. The result was a sea of curricula and heaps of experimental methods, largely untested and lacking hard empirical results, except to establish a larger role for the federal government in educational affairs.

These initiatives soon spilled over into other areas of the curriculum, further removing it from the control of the teacher or even individual boards. It showed little in the way of permanent results as test scores continued to drop. While the Americans were the first on the moon and had historic accomplishments in space, the overall level of science and math proficiency did not increase, but showed steady decline as measured on state, national and international tests.

The impact of such special interest groups, led by professional educators, created a wholesale rewriting of the curriculum. Desks, textbooks, structured periods, teaching methods and, some would argue, discipline, disappeared as the "open classroom", the "Discovery Learning" model and the "Whole Language" approach reached unprecedented levels of acceptance in the nation's schools.

Some of the More Recent Attempts at Reform

The next major shock to the American education system was embodied in President Reagan's *A Nation at Risk* report in 1983. Ironically, Reagan was initially attempting to reduce the role of the federal government in education when this report was commissioned in-house by his Education Secretary, Terrel Bell. According to Toch (1991), the cabinet had rejected a request for a government-sponsored inquiry into the problems of education, and was surprised by the response the initial report evoked. Reagan seized the political moment and became the first "education" president.

A *Nation At Risk* gave rise to the Excellence Movement in education. Reagan skillfully used the need for America to remain globally competitive through better education to draft the leaders of industry and the political right to his cause. In the economic recession of the late 80s, the efforts of CEOs like Apple's John Scully and Chrysler's Lee Iacocca focused public attention on the need for excellence in schools and brought the might of Fortune 500 companies as partners in the teaching process.

The result of this amalgamation between government, business and the schools was the demand for a return to higher standards for both students and teachers. The outcome included an increase in high-school diploma standards in almost every state. Many of these states began requiring more credits in science and math as the minimum standard for graduation. Several states lengthened the school day or the school year. But these reforms were not carried out uniformly across schools and school districts. The schools least affected seemed to be those with the highest illiteracy rates, the largest number of minority students and the least money. (Brookover and Lezotte, 1977)

School Choice and School Restructuring

The two major directions for educational change are school choice and school restructuring. The former involves a number of options, including voucher systems, charter schools, parental choice of schools and homeschooling.

Restructuring has generally been limited to two major types of initiatives: the wholesale restructuring of systems on a district, state or provincial level or the implementation of school-based management programs to devolve the authority and accountability down to the individual school level.

209

Top-Down or Bottom-Up?

The direction of these types of school reformations is as important as the type of intervention. Some attempts are instituted by state, provincial or local politicians and are largely top-down in nature. Others, like some charter schools and homeschooling, originate more in a bottom-up fashion. There are advantages and disadvantages to both directions. The major disadvantage for the top-down approach is that it alienates large numbers of stakeholders and fails to empower many of the individuals who are expected to carry out and maintain the restructuring. It does have the advantage of being able to make sweeping change quickly which can have an immediate impact on the economics and politics of school reform.

The major drawback to the bottom-up approach is that it requires huge amounts of time, effort and consensus-building to get to the point where it becomes an effective voice for change. Its strength may well be in its solidarity and commitment to change, which, although slower, may yield greater results.

Form versus Function

The key objective of any school reform movement, regardless of the type of reform or the method of implementation, is to improve the quality of current education. In almost all cases this is being done by changing the governance, the structure or the funding of education at some level. Very few, if any, reform movements are paying deliberate attention to the process of teaching as part of their reform strategy. The underlying assumption seems to be that the teachers are professionals, and if only the right physical, financial and environmental conditions are established, they will look after the teaching. This assumption is unwarranted, especially for children at risk of school failure.

A Brief Analysis of Major Educational Reform Movements

* *

"Reform comes from below.
No man with four aces asks for a new deal."
- Anon Irishman

Structural Change

The major aim of the structural change reforms is to redesign the governance, funding and/or administration of education by changing the structure of the schools at a local, state, provincial or federal level.

Reform attempts that would fall into this group would include most of the top-down state or provincial government initiatives.

Structural change is also part of some of the bottom-up movements led by parents or educators, such as the Excellence Movement, the Equity Movement and the Charter School Movement. A more extreme example is Homeschooling, where structure is mostly or totally discarded and replaced by instruction at home.

Process Reform Movements

Structural change initiatives have almost completely dominated educational reform. Few educational reformers have come down to the nitty gritty of what will happen in the classroom once the structure has been altered. This level of intervention has apparently been largely left to the teachers and principals. This is the most critical aspect of the intended reforms. With the exception of the Excellence Movement, few have planned for specific details such as the curricular or instructional changes that would accompany the alterations in funding, governance or administration.

Some have made the types of changes that require specific teacher/pupil ratios, specific numbers of courses in English, math or the sciences, mandatory testing and higher standards for graduation, but little or nothing about the process of changing the design or implementation of instruction has been accomplished.

When is Half a Loaf No Better Than None?

These structural changes could have a dramatic impact on the financial and administrative aspects of education and little, if any, on how children are taught.

The question still remains as to what the instructional process will be. To the extent that these processes are ignored or left in the hands of the status quo educators, the changes are unlikely to have any major effect on children's learning and children's literacy.

Getting the structure "right" is half a loaf. But it could wind up being worse than no bread at all. Unless the process is carefully examined to ensure that it will effectively teach the students in this newly structured environment, the reform may represent wasted time, energy and money.

We will review some of the major initiatives from this perspective and comment on some of their strengths and weaknesses.

The Excellence Movement

The publication of A Nation At Risk gave rise to the Excellence Movement and ultimately to the Equity Movement. The former was and still remains an attempt to restore standards and structures to schools which will result in better student performances. The latter attempts to ensure that all schools are treated fairly in terms of the assistance they receive.

The major player in the Excellence Movement is probably the Effective Schools model which originated in Pontiac, Michigan, and spread to Milwaukee and New York in the late seventies. Presently there are approximately 700 schools or school districts involved in the Effective Schools Program (Taylor and Bullard, 1995). This model focuses on having all of the children learn the intended curriculum to a high standard. A compilation of the Effective Schools research outlining over fifteen years of results was published in *Making School Reform Happen* by Bullard and Taylor in 1993.

The Effective Schools philosophy is predicated on seven assumptions outlined in *The Revolution Revisited: Effective Schools and Systemic Reform* (Taylor and Bullard, 1995, pp. 9,10):

1. A clearly stated and focused mission on learning for all.
2. A safe and orderly learning environment.
3. Uncompromising commitment to high expectations for all.
4. Instructional leadership.
5. Optimal opportunity to learn.
6. Frequent monitoring of progress.
7. Enhanced communication.

The authors indicate that the model is not to be considered a quick fix, but a multi-year commitment of shared leadership, power and accountability by all involved. It is not a recipe for change but a set of necessary characteristics to be developed to create long-lasting, effective change.

This prototype is consistent with the Total Quality Management model so effectively used by Deming and MacArthur to rebuild Japan from the rubble of war in 1945 to a superpower twenty-five years later. The Effective Schools model is the educational equivalent of Deming's industrial principles.

One of the strengths of the Excellence Model is that it does pay close attention to both the structure and the process

of educational reform, including the need to change instruction. It takes account of what will be taught and how it will be
taught, without dictating a specific methodology. There is a
great deal of emphasis on common agreement and in having
each of the stakeholders committed to the objectives and the
process of change. As expected, this process is deliberate and
consumes the time and energies of all parties involved, from
parents to top school officials.

The movement has been criticized for being too ill-defined
and for having schools pick and choose some, but not all, of
the seven key objectives, and specialize in changing only those
selected. Despite these criticisms, the Excellence Movement
may be the best hope for real reform within the existing public school scene, although it is likely to have less effect in areas
where children live in poverty and are at highest risk of school
failure.

The movement has been successful with inner-city, predominantly poor African-American students in schools in St.
Louis, Missouri, immigrant children in Seattle, poor kids in
Spanish Harlem and students in other lower socio-economic
settings. It is, however, a movement supported more widely by
middle-class parents concerned for their children's education.
This is not a criticism of the Excellence Movement because it
appears to be equally true of the broad spectrum of educational reformers. It simply means that it may be more difficult and
time-consuming to effect educational change in areas where
there are fewer leadership resources than may be found in
many predominantly white middle-class neighborhoods.

In their 1995 book, Taylor and Bullard outline the philosophy and the progress of the Excellence Movement over the
last decade. As examples of its effectiveness, they report major
case studies of the Effective Education process in school districts in Spring Branch, Texas; St. John's, Florida; Springfield,
Massachusetts; and Glendale, Arizona.

The School Equity Movement

The reforms of the Excellence Movement, which again

were largely the concerns of middle-class America, bypassed many underprivileged schools and led directly to the next attempt at reform. The Equity Movement attempted to redistribute resources within education. This thrust was an effort by some educators to restore the balance of funding to lower socio-economic schools and their students. To some degree, while they have been successful at least in terms of securing more funding, the results do not reflect widespread increases in performance emanating from these schools.

The Charter School Movement

Charter Schools are independent public schools. They operate by obtaining a charter from their school district or from some politically empowered officials. This allows them to run an independent school which is fully funded by the local board or whoever is in charge of educational funding for the area. Charter schools are based on a contract by a group of teachers, parents, or other interested parties who wish autonomy from the school district, its regulations and policies. Typically, a charter school has a contract for three to five years which outlines the responsibilities for which they will be held accountable. The new charter school is usually free of state education departments, teacher unions and associations, and local school administrators. It has a board of directors made up of teachers, parents and often some public school board official who together are ultimately responsible for the charter and fulfilling its mandate.

Charter schools are not private schools. They do not and cannot charge tuition. They receive the same funding as other public schools in the district in which they are founded. Many charter schools have been started by teachers who wish to have more freedom and are willing to accept more stringent accountability for educational results.

Creating a Charter School

Charter Schools began in Minnesota in 1986 when some

parents were unable to get their local school board to provide a kindergarten program for their children. They took their case to the state legislature and obtained a charter to do so from the governor. Minnesota passed the first Charter School legislation in the USA. Since then, over half of the states of the nation and one Canadian province (Alberta) have enacted similar bills. Other Canadian provinces and U.S. states are considering following suit.

Generally a charter is obtained by an interested group after they have submitted a proposal. The proposal outlines in detail the organization and specific plans for their school to the sponsor who is responsible for granting charters. Should the proposal not be accepted by the sponsor, there is usually an appeal mechanism for the chartering group.

Such schools have arisen from the frustration and lack of flexibility public boards have shown in meeting the needs of parents and in some cases, teachers.

Problems with Charter Schools

The major problem with charter schools to this point is found in the legislation by which they are created. In a number of cases, the existing educational lobbyists, unions and other interest groups have been able to force amendments to the charter legislation which effectively gut it. Legislators have had compromises forced upon them by the educational establishment which lead to the passage of very weak charter school legislation. As a result, few, if any, charters are granted. While there is the appearance of there being charter school options, they are, in fact, almost non-existent. According to Freedman (1996), this situation has occurred in states such as Georgia and Kansas. Freedman refers to charter school legislation as being either "live", meaning that it provides real autonomy and accountability, such as in California, Arizona and Michigan, or "dead", meaning that the legislation is on the books, but is having little, if any, effect on the formation of charter schools.

Homeschooling

It is estimated that over one million North American school-aged children are being taught at home with the parent(s) acting as teachers or supervisors of learning activities. Generally, the reason why parents choose to educate their children at home is rooted in strong philosophical or religious beliefs. Many point to concerns over the declining quality of public education as the number one reason for choosing this alternative to traditional schooling. Homeschooling parents argue that teaching their children at home strengthens family ties and provides for quality academic instruction tailored to the students' needs and abilities. It also ensures safety and selective socialization. (Ironically, the major criticism of homeschooling is the isolation of children from peer interaction.) Flexible time permits intensive study in an area of student interest for the more gifted learner or additional time for the child with learning difficulties. Regulations governing homeschooling vary from state to state, province to province, but generally there are mechanisms in place to cover registration, testing, curriculum and teaching materials. A limited survey of current research suggests that homeschooled children are frequently top achievers, performing above state or provincial scores of non-homeschooled students. A growing number of groups provide support to parents and children in homeschooling situations in terms of networking, curricular design and resource materials.

The School Council Movement

Among the last wave of reforms to impact schools in the past decade has been the School Council Movement. State, provincial or municipal governments have created school councils with varying degrees of power in an attempt to return some accountability to the local school and community.

The arrangement replaces or augments existing school boards with school councils and expands the role of the councils from advisory to governance. The thrust is to create less central administration and less dependence on a government

Ministry or Department of Education.

Those in favor of school councils maintain that decisions would be more in line with local needs and would reflect local diversity better at less expense and with more efficiency. There is not yet sufficient data to bear out these claims, but some states and provinces, especially Ontario, Quebec and New Brunswick, have either moved or are moving in this direction.

Perhaps the most notable Canadian experiment in school councils is to be found in New Brunswick. In 1996, Frank McKenna, the then-premier of this Atlantic province, abolished school boards in favor of school councils. These councils were comprised of appointees who were to make decisions regarding education for the province. The result has been far less than favorable, with groups of parents and taxpayers on the verge of revolt. Recently, the province's education minister resigned and the entire program is now being given a hard second look.

Jurisdictions seem to choose between school councils and charter schools. Rarely do they have both.

Merit Pay Initiatives

Another reform attempt that has found favor in the last decade is based on the idea of merit pay. This is a systematic attempt to reward competent teachers or schools with extra money and not reward those who do not produce predetermined academic results. The idea was borrowed from the business world where staff and executives are given bonuses or perks for reaching quotas, production levels, quality control standards or some specific objective. The measures used to determine the production of learning, however, are less clear than most business targets. As a result, there is some degree of arbitrariness in most merit-pay systems which can create major problems. Ladd (1996) describes the experiences of several districts with merit-pay initiatives, including the one which follows.

The South Carolina Experience

As part of its 1984 Education Improvement Act, South Carolina instituted a number of steps aimed at improving school performance. They increased teacher pay, added higher graduation requirements, began a universal kindergarten program, adopted an exit exam for high school seniors, provided performance incentives for principals, made possible elected school-improvement councils, added more special education testing and resources and allotted more capital expenditures. This increase in educational spending was supported by a 1% increase in the state sales tax that resulted in a 20% increase in educational revenues.

Testing and Payoffs

To track the effects of these steps, all students were tested annually to see the if actual academic change matched the expected one-year gain over a school year. The results were collected and students who were not enrolled for the full year were dropped from the data. Rewards to the schools were based on the "gains" of the students as measured by these standardized tests.

But it was feared that the gains from standardized tests would not accurately reflect what was actually happening. For example, test scores for weaker students might not rise as quickly as those of stronger students and would always remain below the expected increase. Very strong students might not have had enough room left for advancement because of their already high scores and would be limited by a "ceiling effect" of the tests.

The weaker students also happened to be students from poor and often non-white areas and would make up the bulk of some schools' students. Their slower growth would eliminate their schools from ever receiving the rewards, despite their best efforts.

The gains were based on the change in the medians of the test scores from one year to the next. Since the median score is the one which splits the distribution in half, a change in it would more accurately reflect a change in all of the children. This was done to keep teachers from optimizing the performances of their top students and using a mean, an average derived by dividing the total gain by the number of students.

The South Carolina plan paid off 25% of the schools with rewards. But in order to give each school what was believed to be a more equal chance, the formula was changed to account for socio-economic conditions. A factor was included to account for students who qualified for free-lunch programs, another for reduced-price lunches, another for the relative teaching experience of the classroom teacher, another for children entering school with pre-first grade entry skills.

Each of these factors creates further complexity in determining winners and losers. As the measurements become more complicated, fewer and fewer of those involved are likely to understand them. If it is seen to be administered unfairly or in a way teachers and parents do not fully comprehend, the school's $15,000 - $20,000 payoff can become the source of problems, not the solution that was intended.

When schools work hard, see an increase in the test scores and do not get any reward because the convoluted formula has ranked other schools above them, there is a tendency toward dissension. Many decide not to participate as completely as they might because they feel that they can't win anyway.

An alternative approach to using standardized tests as a basis of school performance could be to use Ogden Lindsley's measurement technology, Precision Teaching. It does answer a number of the issues in the merit pay approach to changing school performance. It has been successfully used at a school system and state level and is resistant to corruption, socio-economic variables and the disparity associated with different amounts of teacher experience.

The Houston Payoff

Merit pay for individual teachers has also been tried. The Houston Independent School District used a teacher rather than school merit-pay program. They had many of the same issues on deriving a formula that would equalize opportunity for the teachers. Individual merit pay systems can be an equally fractious approach. Trying to create a level playing field is a very difficult problem. If one teacher feels that he is being treated unfairly because of being given a less than perfect group of kids, a poor timetable or insufficient supplies or support, it can mean that a real failure to cooperate can result.

Summary

Education is in flux. A number of different restructuring options are being advocated and implemented in various jurisdictions. There is not a great mass of data to support choosing one option over another to this point. Much of the available data is being ignored or attacked. For those who have concerns about our children's education, the landscape can quickly become very confusing. We ask ourselves "What's a body to do?"

What's a Body to Do?

● ●

"Don't Fix the Blame. Fix the Problem."
- Japanese Saying

The Problem

There is a huge problem in our schools. Students are not receiving quality education. Millions are leaving to join the adult world ill-prepared. Many of them are illiterate. Our schools are creating failure at an unacceptable and unprecedented rate. In an information age, it is extremely difficult to be a fully participating member of society when you cannot read or write well or at all.

Reformers of many stripes have leapt into the fray. Some are special-interest groups protecting their turf; some are politically motivated, using schools to promote their own particular point of view. Most of them have yet to conclude that it's what happens when the teacher closes the classroom door that is going to make the crucial difference. And in too many classrooms, not enough is happening behind that closed door.

Many of those leading or influencing the reforms are the same people who have created the problem and who have mismanaged the school systems for the past 50 years. They are administrators, bureaucrats, consultants and other hangers-on who have come to be the fox guarding the chicken house. They do not come to us with clear options. They ignore replicated, effective research and make an emotional appeal to our concern for children. They promise a new day in education with almost total ignorance of what actually works. Their case is pure rhetoric.

The educational media has been of little help. Their coverage and promotion of just about anything new that comes down the pike has resulted in little more than added confusion to an already disoriented situation. They have not held school systems up to that close scrutiny reserved for rock stars and princesses. With the exception of a couple of columnists, they have yet to figure out the story line.

The Solution

The solution to the literacy and school failure problem is writ large in the educational research of the past 30 years. It leaps off the pages of Project Follow Through. It snaps your head up in the Sacajawea study. In setting after setting where effective methods are employed judiciously, the results are undeniable and irrefutable. The data speak volumes. When the teaching fails, the at-risk student fails. Improve the teaching. . .

Literacy as a Civil Rights' Issue

Every North American has the right to an effective education. Any failure of schools to teach someone to read is a violation of his right to be an informed citizen of that society.

It may be that we subscribe to some of the methods used by other civil-rights activists. This approach may be used by one person - the Rosa Parks of non-readers, refusing to be treated as a second-class citizen - or by groups of parents in letter writing campaigns and presentations at meetings at all levels within an educational system.

The following suggestions may be of some assistance to prepare people interested in creating change.

Be Knowledgeable

If you don't have the power to mandate the change you want, you must find a way to convince the powers at hand to do what you wish. The best weapon in this battle is hard data. You must gather the facts - the empirical data which support your position and those which repudiate the opposition's. You must learn their arguments, their points of view and you must be able to rebut their position convincingly. There is a list of suggested readings in the Appendix. If a parent, teacher or taxpayer hones their skills and learns what works, what doesn't and what changes are needed, they will be much more effective advocates for those who cannot gather and use this information for themselves. You can make a difference, but as Bob Dylan says, "I must know the song well before I start singing."

The Challenge

The challenge is in getting schools, subject specialists, school boards, trustees, state and provincial education departments to accept and use effective programs, especially in the primary grades. This is not anywhere as easy as it sounds. Even if everyone from top to bottom in the elementary grades of a school district opted to implement an effective set of instructional programs like Direct Instruction, or measurement practices like Precision Teaching, they are faced with an awesome task. If you were sufficiently fortunate to find the teacher, the principal and the supervisors who have the authority to implement such programs to be totally agreeable and ready to act, there would still be much to do.

Issues

Given that the teacher is going to have to change his teaching methods, other issues in the classroom need to be resolved. The classroom has to be well-organized with additional seatwork and other activities provided for the students not currently being instructed. There will be a lot of work produced by fast-learning students which needs to be corrected and returned reasonably promptly.

The teachers would require training and supervision. The

program will only be as good as the skills the teacher brings to the task and those come only from adequate training. Such training is arduous and demanding. There are numerous instances where schools have bought the materials but have not had the teachers trained. The program does not get the expected results and is abandoned as not being helpful.

After the training, the teacher's classroom performance needs to be monitored on a regular basis with constructive, corrective feedback provided by a qualified supervisor who has a thorough knowledge of the technology. This takes a great deal of time and creates a further problem - there are relatively few trainers or supervisors who have the skills to train and monitor the teacher-training program.

It takes a significant amount of time and practice to develop the skills of a trainer. It is probably impossible to train sufficient teachers, establish a sufficient number of programs and monitor them properly to remediate the reading skills of every child in a district or even in a school immediately. The process of responding to this huge need is like eating an elephant.

Eating the Elephant

Hospitals dealing with a catastrophe use a process called triage. Triage is aimed to stabilize the situation as rapidly as possible with the fewest casualties. A version of it could be used here. In a first pass, our triage could start with a very quick analysis of the children in the primary grades who may be at risk of school failure. This is not a difficult task. Simply see if they can read a passage quickly and easily from a Grade Three reader in a one-minute timed reading, or use a Direct Instruction program placement test. If the student reads fewer than 200 words per minute, or exceeds the placement test error limit, he becomes an immediate candidate for remediation. These are the walking wounded. Children with reading rates around 100 words per minute or more frequent placement test errors are at greater risk. These are litter cases. Any child who cannot read above 60 words per minute or tests at the beginning of the reading series is a critical care casualty.

Call for medivac!

Once you have a rough idea of who has what degree of reading problem, you can begin to group the children for instruction and set your remediation priorities. Select the students who will be given priority for the first program(s). These are likely the non-readers or the poorest readers in Grade 3 who will not receive an appropriate level of reading instruction in the coming grades. Set up only as many programs for which you have the capacity to train and monitor teachers. Doing remediation badly will only generate the kinds of remedial results we are seeing in schools today. Get these started and give them precedence over the rest of the curriculum. If a well-trained teacher completes a Direct Instruction reading lesson each school day, the students will be reading by the end of the year.

Now we can begin to make plans for the next step. Once we have survived triage, we can adopt more far-reaching remedial and preventative measures. The process is begun, the first bite digested.

The Reality

It is far more likely that any suggestion, request or demand for more effective programs in schools is going to be met with opposition. Teachers are generally very testy about being told how or what to teach, even when some of them are generating next year's special-education candidates. Principals do not take kindly to being asked to implement specific programs, unless it is by their director or superintendent. Requests by parents are most often not implemented into the classroom, so if changes are going to occur, it will probably only be after a fairly strenuous fight.

Although schools will say that they are open to suggestions and want parents to participate, they generally do not mean in terms of looking at the effectiveness of the teaching or any changes to it.

Like most professionals, teachers are territorial and will fight for their turf, even against the parents of the children they teach, or fail to teach. Teachers, principals and the rest of the educational hierarchy subscribe to theories of teaching. These theories are usually just that - theories. But many educators act as if they were written on tablets of stone and brought down from the mountain. This is another instance of theories getting in the way of progress rather than fostering it. This is largely true because the theory has little or no evidence to support it. It may sound logical or rational or good for kids but it just doesn't work. Or at least it cannot demonstrate that it works in any objective way. But the theory is still believed, even when it is hurting the kids. And it is truly a question of belief because there is no proof one way or the other. The theory acts as a set of blinders and closes the minds of its proponents. To the extent that this situation occurs, parents can be in for a long and wearing battle to convince educators to change.

Forming the Interest Group

One of the very early strategies is to try never to fight alone. Find allies. Sometimes the parent-teacher association at the school level is a good place to start. Be careful. Not all parents are alert to curriculum issues. They intentionally leave that domain to the teachers. You can get a pretty good read on the group's thinking by finding out what type of agenda issues have been part of their past meetings. If they are more interested in playground equipment or school trips, they are useful allies for the school but they may be of little use to you.

Check into groups such as:

The International Institute for Advocacy for School Children (I'ASC)
296 W. 8th Ave.,
Eugene, Oregon
97401
Ph. (541) 485-6349

This group has been dealing with the prevention of academic child abuse, a form of neglect which is created in schools where children are not provided the foundation skills that will allow them to be successful in an educational environment. Their information, especially their report on *Academic Child Abuse* (Bateman), could form the basis for a discussion on reading concerns in any school.

Start with a sign-up sheet for a discussion group on your school's reading levels and see who is interested. Call them and set up the first meeting, preferably at the school.

Once the interest group has come together, it is critical that they determine the agenda and agree on it. Keep the agenda simple, one or two things you want to accomplish first is all you need for now. Expect to lose some members. Unless and until the group has a consensus on what it's about, it is likely to splinter under the pressure. The group doesn't need to be large, but it does need to be cohesive.

Some Possible Aims for the Group

1. To determine the current level of reading skills of the students in a class, school, district.
2. To determine existing methods of reading instruction which are effective with new and/or problem readers.
3. To advocate the adoption of effective reading programs for all of the school's children.
4. To establish effective reading programs for every child in the school, beginning in the primary grades.
5. To reduce any problems of students who are non-readers by 50% within one academic year through effectively taught and measurable remedial programs.
6. To reduce the problem of any students who are poor readers by 50% within one academic year through effectively taught and measurable programs.
7. To ensure that all students are competent readers by the end of the second grade.
8. To continuously monitor the school's performance on basic teaching skills and make such information available for the benefit of all concerned.

Once the aims are clearly stated, recorded and agreed upon, the work can begin. Different members of the group will arrive with different experience, different skills, and different amounts of time and energy. Leaders will generally emerge and tasks and roles can be assigned to maximize the potential of the group without duplicating anyone's efforts.

The Newsletter, Electronic or Otherwise

In any struggle, information is a powerful ally. Things that are written on paper or seen on a computer bulletin board are often perceived to be more believable than those which are not. The existence of a newsletter also adds a sense of permanence and substance to the group's efforts. It is a record that you can point to as a history in future meetings. A newsletter allows other parents to see what you are doing now and what you are planning next. It extends your reach into the school community, may allow a voice for individuals in and outside of the group and it may bring you more concerned parents to assist you. In some instances, an on-line newsletter could be established. Accessible by computer, it would eliminate the need for frequent direct contact. Combined with e-mail, a website could add a great deal of power to your cause.

Setting Out a Plan

With consensus achieved and some basic housekeeping done, the group can begin to determine how it intends to get the teacher, school or district to accept its advice and institute an effective program. It is important to have each member become knowledgeable about what works in reading programs. Having divided up, reviewed and presented back to the group the relevant literature, the defense of its position and the points on which the opposition may be vulnerable, the group is ready to talk to the school.

The meetings should be carefully scheduled to ensure the attendance of the teacher and/or the principal you wish to address. The first meetings may be between individual parents and their children's respective teachers. The following questions can be asked:

1. What does my child know now?
2. What will you teach him next?
3. How will you know that he knows it?
4. How will I know that he knows it?

It is important to get answers to these questions. Do not leave the meeting without having them answered to your complete satisfaction or at very least, having another meeting set up to get the answers. You may have to ask the same question several times in order to get an answer. Be polite but persistent.

Being Proactive

With educators, as with bureaucrats, never leave a meeting without having scheduled the next one. Doing this lets them know that you are serious. The next gathering should not be more than a couple of weeks from the first one. Once a teacher knows that you will be returning periodically to get answers to specific questions, you will get a different response than most parents get.

You can also go to the meeting with personal information about your child's reading. Have the child read aloud to you or to someone who reads well for a period of sixty seconds. The passage can be from his reader or from a library book. Count the number of errors he makes and the number of words read. Errors include words that are miscalled, omitted, or ones that are inserted but do not appear in the text. Count the total number of words, subtract the errors and see how many words your child read correctly in one minute. If the score is between two hundred and two hundred and fifty with no more than two errors, your child is a fluent reader. If it is less than that, your child has a reading problem that is in direct proportion to the distance of his current score from 200 - 250 words per minute.

Read the passage aloud yourself and see how your score

compares. Although it sounds like a lot, reading two hundred words per minute correctly is a comfortable reading rate for non-technical material.

Collect as much of the reading data as you can and analyze it so that you can talk intelligently about the parents' findings. Be prepared to be told that such data are not really valid or useful in determining whether or not your child is a good reader.

The first argument will likely be that reading fast is unnecessary and possibly undesirable. I would ask the principal or teacher how fast a child should read and then offer them samples by reading aloud to them so that they can appreciate what different reading rates sound like. Try reading to them at 60 words per minute and you will likely get some agreement that there is a desirable rate at which to get the words off the page. Now what remains is to agree on what the range of reading rates should be. See how the children stack up to that benchmark at the present time. If that tack fails to get some agreement on reading fluencies, try reading to the meeting at 30 words per minute. They will eventually get the picture.

The next standard defense you are likely to hear is that reading fluently does not mean that the child understands a thing about what he has just read. Absolutely true. Reading comprehension is another set of skills in the domain of reading. But first you must at least be able to get the words off the page with reasonable speed and accuracy. If you can't do that much, how are you ever going to understand what you have read? So begin with just reading the words properly as a first step. At least you have a starting point for doing something about changing the reading abilities of the children.

Possible Excuses

It's time now to open the discussion about the current state of reading in the class, school or district and what the teacher, principal or superintendent intends to do about it. This is the point where children take it on the chin. The school officials will almost certainly trot out all of the reasons

why some children don't (can't) learn to read. Listen carefully to hear anything that indicates that the instruction is flawed
or that the school is in any way responsible. You will most likely hear everything except that. The kids are from broken
homes, are dyslexic, have ADHD (attention deficit, hyperactivity disorder), are unmotivated, whatever - you can be pretty sure the problem is going to be pinned on something other
than the school or the teaching.

The best defense is the data from programs where similar
children have learned despite these inhibiting conditions or
learning histories. The data from Follow Through, Sacajawea,
QLC, Morningside, Ben Bronz Academy, the Haughton
Learning Center, the Cache Valley Learning Center, the Wesley Elementary School in Houston, the SPEED School in
Chicago are all good case studies which suggest specific, data-
based options for reading improvement.

You are likely to have a distinct advantage in this part of
the discussion if you have done your homework. Most school
officials, especially as you go up the chain of command, are
usually unwittingly ignorant of programs that work. They may
be caught a little flat-footed in their defense simply because
they have not read as much research as you have. Not having
the data will cause them little problem. They are used to working without it. Your specific knowledge of particularly effective
programs could give you an advantage. Use your advantage to
get a survey of present reading skills done with the promise of
a pilot program for at least some of the children at risk.

The School's Existing Reading Program

The next most likely defense from the school's side is that
they already have a program that works for *most* of the children. Certainly they will admit to having some problem readers, but that happens because of some genetic or environmental deficit for which the school should not be held accountable. In their view, you should understand and accept this.
They are well aware of the problem and are addressing it and
things certainly are better now than they were a while ago.

This is a good time to ask for the reading data for the school. There probably won't be any, or they will not be current. Their availability is not likely to be a major concern of administration. Data requests from parents are usually dismissed by school administrators as something the teachers are already doing (but not making available for public consumption) or something that is specialized and left up to the school psychologists and others who use eduspeak. You'll probably be told that parents should simply trust the school.

Stall Tactics

Finally yielding to a request for testing is most likely the school's next step. Oftentimes this simply means that they are pulling out of their listening posts and regrouping in the forward trenches for the coming battle. They now know you are serious and that they will indeed have to defend their turf. Delaying tactics often become an effective weapon for the school.

Such testing almost never happens immediately. Budgets, timetables, availability of the people who will do the evaluation, and several dozen other factors can turn the process into a retirement project. I have seen hundreds of cases where, after several meetings with the parents, the school finally collapses and agrees to an assessment of the child/ren. Routinely, the assessment is months away, and the results are almost never known until close to the end of that school year. The parents and child have spent a year in limbo. This is where you need the patience of Job and the tenacity of a pit bull. When the testing is finally done, the results are often translated by the school in such a way as to deny assistance immediately because of insufficient resources, long waiting lists, more pressing problems of other parents and so on. This may also be the point at which you are forced to move the issue to the next level of administration. This is also the time when it is good not to be a single set of parents trying to solve the problem. The upper levels of school administrations understand numbers better than they understand most individual requests or arguments.

Meeting the Higher Levels

If your concerns have not been adequately met at the school level by the teachers, principal or reading specialists, the next stop is at the school district level. Once you reach the levels of administration above the individual school, you have to become much like a consultant. You must be able to make a presentation that outlines the current problem. Then you need to be able to propose a solution for which you already have a plan and which has proven itself in the past. Such a plan must carry little, if any, risk for the upper management to adopt. The risk to them is in not adopting a proven method while endorsing or being seen to endorse methods that are non-productive. This is where the short, well-organized presentation of the history of effective methods and the promise of solving a major problem can be appealing to school administrators. They must also get the message that should they be unwilling to assist you in solving this problem, you are prepared to take the matter to the school board of trustees. The concept of academic child abuse may be helpful in this context and should be carefully explained to them.

Sometimes you may find one or two allies at this level of management, usually a few who are trying to make a mark so they can scale the professional heights. They can be very useful if they have the power or can influence the powers that make the decisions. It's generally a good idea to see that they get some credit or profile from these activities to help them in their upward passage. A mention of their assistance in your newsletter is a good place to start. If, in fact, the entire group remains unmoved by your efforts, take the discussion to the next level, the elected board of trustees.

The Board Presentation

This is a point at which this information could first be picked up by the press who routinely cover such meetings. It literally is showtime. Usually presentations to the board by any interested group are a part of the board's open public meeting. In most instances there is a time limit, usually ten to

234

fifteen minutes. The group has to be well-organized. The presentation has to hit the mark. Outline the problem, describe the options and get a commitment to do something.

These meetings are also sparsely attended. As mentioned previously, only 2% of parents ever go to a school board meeting. It's a good idea to pack the house if you can. Bring as many people as you can rally. This impresses the trustees who are used to looking at empty chairs. These attendees are also voters and the press may be interested. One possibility is to come away with an agreement for a pilot project in a school that has not shown good reading scores. Try to pick a school where the staff is generally cooperative and the principal is not threatened by your attempts to improve his school.

Starting a Pilot Program in Reading

The changes that any concerned group of parents or school supporters expects to make are definitely not going to happen overnight. If you can convince the system to implement a pilot program of an effective method, you have won your first major battle. You now have the thin edge of the wedge inserted. A great deal of focus should now be given to driving it home.

Any pilot program will need to be carefully monitored to see that it is properly implemented. If a pilot program is established, it could be done in such a way that it will fail despite its ability to produce the desired results. Some programs have been started without the proper training of the teacher, or without supervision by anyone who knows how to review the progress and problems faced by the teacher. The methods advocated here are specific technologies with specific procedures. If they are not followed, it will impact the results in direct proportion to the degree to which they were not followed.

There is not much point in fighting hard to get a program started and then not check up on its implementation to see that it is being done by the numbers. It would not take very long for an intelligent parent who was visiting the classroom periodically to discern whether or not the program was being properly run.

Parents could also be of great help in implementing a reading program. There are almost always too few people to listen to the children read. Any assistance from parent volunteers helps to lighten the teacher's load and will usually be much appreciated. It is also a good way to see what is happening in the classroom.

If, for whatever reason, the program is not being properly set up or monitored, it is critical that the group acts immediately. A badly-run program fails to help the students and damages the credibility of those sponsoring it.

What if the Board Won't Act

If you leave the board meeting with no guarantee of action, there are official channels you should pursue next. These are regional, state or other authorities to whom these people report, and from whom they may derive some or all of their money for some or all of their programs. Soon you will be up to your eyeballs in bureaucrats. That can really slow you down and can cause you major fits of anger and depression. The bureaucracy is one more step removed from the problem and has one more layer of protection for its actions or inaction. They are also usually more adept at handling discontented groups or individuals because it goes with the territory. Expect progress to be slow. If you can get these people on your side, you have won a major victory. If they also turn out to be intransigent, your efforts will have to be doubled and redoubled over a considerably longer period of time. Look on each of these exercises as raising the bar. The local school administration and board know that they have a formidable opponent on their hands, one who is well-organized and determined. You are not some group who shows up, makes its case and, having been heard and turned down, is dismissed and disperses into the night. This is the fate of most of the groups they deal with. Don't let it be yours.

Options

It may be at this point that you realize that any help is like-ly to come too late for your son or daughter. The struggle to make changes may go on for an extended period, but your child can no longer wait for that help to arrive.

This is when many parents begin to seek options inside or outside of their public board. The usual options within their existing board are:

1. Placing the student in a new classroom or program within the existing school.
2. Moving to another public school in the same district.
3. Having the child repeat the grade.
4. Living with the problem.

None of these options is guaranteed to change anything except to have your child get a year older. Unless the new pro-gram or class has a star teacher with a proven track record, the parent has no better idea of the likelihood of success than before. Changing schools falls into the same category. Having the child repeat the grade is also no guarantee that he will receive anything better in the way of instruction than he did the year before. The child also pays a price in repeating a grade level. The price is personal because the child can hardly not see this as failure - *his* personal failure. The cost is social - most or all of his classmates move up a grade while he remains behind and has to explain why. The cost is emotional. Although that may vary from child to child, it's bound to be there. The cost is even potentially financial in that it takes away another year of his working life.

The options that exist outside of the public schools are:

1. Continuing to fight the battle at other levels of bureaucracy.
2. Joining other groups or associations to become part of a bigger entity.
3. Changing to another system.
4. Enrolling in a private school.

5. Enrolling at a Christian school or other denominational school.
6. Starting a charter school.
7. Getting tutorial help.
8. Attending summer schools at a learning center or camp.
9. Choosing homeschooling.

Exercising the Options

As the time for assistance for their child's academic problems appears to fade further and further into the future, many parents may become discouraged and less and less involved. That plays into the hands of the status quo and does little to promote change or get help for their own student(s). Parents may exercise one or more of the options listed above. They have to make their own decision with the resources they have available.

Stop-Gap Measures

As with most problems, the preferred solution is the one which will add the minimum critical cost in terms of time, effort, money and disruption in order to get the maximum gain. Effective help from within the school is the easiest solution; tutoring from other sources outside of school hours is probably the next easiest but has greater cost; changing schools is usually more disruptive in terms of time and inconvenience and may not even be an option in non-urban areas. Sometimes it also adds tuition costs. Private schools do tend to be expensive and should be seen as almost a final option. Just because they are private does not automatically mean that they are an answer to your difficulty. Check them out as carefully as any other school.

If your state or province has legislation which allows parents to sue school boards for non-performance, you might wish to investigate that option. Litigation, however, is almost always more costly and time-consuming than you could ever expect. You could wind up spending as much for a lawyer as you would have for tuition in a fine private school and still not have a solution. It is more the threat of a suit, especially one brought and funded by a group of parents that will make school officials sit up and take notice. Do not exercise this option lightly and do so only if the legislation is in place to provide you some relief.

Extra Help

While you are waiting for the school to act, you might consider getting some extra help for your child(ren) in after-school tutorials. The school may offer homework clubs or extra instruction after class. If you can avail yourself of any of these services, you should try them. You need to monitor these assists to see what, if any, effect they are having. You could ask the instructor the same four questions that are listed earlier in this chapter. If, in a few weeks, you see no measurable improvement in specific skills, you may need to look else-where.

One choice is a tutor. There are retired teachers who are taking a few students into their homes and helping them after school for a reasonable fee. Check them out. Get references of past and present clients. Call them to see how helpful the experience has been for their child. Ask the set of questions to the tutor as you did at the school. Look for anyone who offers you some hard data about your child's performance on a week-ly basis.

Another choice is a learning center. Again you must exer-cise good judgment. Learning centers have overheads to be met and are usually run as a business. Many of their founders and/or managers have a background in education, but that in and of itself is no insurance that they will solve your child's academic difficulty. Make sure that you are not merely con-tributing to someone's bottom line. Again, ask the questions and write down their answers. Listen carefully for how success will be measured and who will take responsibility for the learn-ing. Remember - if the student didn't learn, the teacher didn't teach. No other explanation will suffice. Get references and check them out. See if they will provide a guarantee as the centers using our technologies do. Don't just pick the place because of a glitzy magazine or television ad. One of the largest of the international companies in the tutoring business does a masterful job of marketing its services, but I am not personally impressed with its academic program. Look beyond the facade. Get a solid idea of what any tutor will deliver and the timelines within which you can expect the objectives to be accomplished. If you're not satisfied, continue shopping.

Changing Schools

Changing schools sometimes works. If it allows your child to escape a known, ineffective teacher, it is probably worth considering. It can be a major disruption, especially if the parents have to take on the transportation of the child. The new school may not turn out to be any more effective. Again, screen the teacher and principal by asking the four questions. Whether the new school is in the public system, is a denominational school, an alternative school or a private school, it should be held up to close and continuous scrutiny if you are going to give them your offspring. Kids only go through school once, so there is some urgency to get it right.

Computers and the Internet

Sometimes parents conclude that if their child had a computer, he would do better at school. The computer is just another tool. The educational software that is available is often very splashy, with great graphics and few results. The computer is in line to catch a lot of blame for not making kids smart. It is another of those hopeful, rhetorical arguments made in education without the benefit of empirical results.

As an educator, I have searched for effective educational software. I found so little that we finally created our own, *Mighty Math* and *Math Tutor*, marketed worldwide by Scholastic of New York. These math programs do keep records and advance the student only after the he demonstrates competency on the present lesson. The fact that they won international awards and have remained in the marketplace without upgrades for a dozen years does say something about their ability to teach kids math. Unless a computer program can offer the same benefits as a good teacher or tutor, it is not likely to provide a satisfactory solution. The computer is not the educational panacea some people would have you believe it to be. Look for results, not tools.

CyberSlate.ca

As mentioned in Chapter 12, there is an Internet service which is currently in development that will be of assistance. It is called CyberSlate.ca and is being launched on the Net sometime in late 1998. With the help of the Research Council of Canada, it will soon be available to students everywhere. It is currently in an embryonic stage and will initially offer only a limited set of programs. Plans are now being drawn to expand the offerings across the entire curriculum in the coming months and years. CyberSlate will provide the kinds of data-based programs that will allow the parent and the learner to determine progress at the touch of a key.

Becoming The Teacher

If the school system is unable to provide a solution for your child's problem in becoming competent in basic literacy and numeracy skills, and if you cannot derive satisfaction from other available services, you may wish to start your own literacy program. Any individual or a group of parents is certainly capable of becoming a competent reading, spelling or math teacher. All of the tools required to teach any of the skills needed by children in the elementary grades can be learned by any intelligent person, given a good trainer. The training is available in a number of places.

Zig Engelmann and his colleagues have been hosting the Direct Instruction Conference annually every August in

Eugene, Oregon, for almost thirty years. You don't have to be a teacher to go. You will learn everything you need to know to teach at least some of the Direct Instruction programs. In a couple of summers you could be an effective teacher. Training is also available in Canada. The Second Annual Direct Instruction conference was held in Toronto in August, 1998, and will hopefully continue for many more years. There is another regional Direct Instruction conference in Utah each year.

Kent Johnson and Morningside Learning Systems provide training in Seattle at their annual Summer Institute. Ogden Lindsley has been closely associated with these sessions during the past several years. This training offers both Direct Instruction and Precision Teaching. It also demonstrates the instructional design innovations developed at Morningside.

Ogden Lindsley has also been offering pre-conference workshops for beginning Precision Teachers as part of the Annual Association for Behavior Analysis international conference. This conference is held during the last week of May each year in one of the major cities across the U.S.

Check Out Your Community-Based Literacy Services

Most communities also have some form of literacy council or literacy services. These are often run by volunteers and are non-profit community agencies. Like the schools, they are usually either unaware or unconcerned about the more effective methods found in the literature. Given that their mandate is to assist the illiterate, it is somewhat reasonable to expect them to be on the lookout for effective programs. Like public schools however, the community funding that these groups receive is not based on performance, but on their status as a non-profit agency. Often these organizations are financially supported, at least in part, by grants. Community funding agencies like the United Way are often involved. If future funding were made contingent on demonstrating success with their clients, there might be more impetus for literacy groups to seek out and use the most effective programs available. This will likely happen only if the granting body asks the right questions.

Many literacy groups are reliant on volunteers as tutors or teachers, so the training task would be a significant challenge and would likely be an ongoing process. The additional successes at the end of the day should make the investment of time, money and effort worthwhile. Another way in which you can assist is to join your local literacy group and bring the information about what works to their attention with the request that they learn as much as possible about implementing such methods.

If You Build It, They Will Come

During the past twenty years, I have spent a part of my time building learning centers based on the QLC model for myself and others. Some of the success stories reported in this book began by copying our original system, refining it and adding improvements. All of these learning center practitioners are in the world of private enterprise, selling the technologies to parents and agencies for literally millions of dollars - technologies we cannot convince the public schools to use. Some of our learning centers have become registered private schools offering full-time academic programs.

All of us are anxious to see our numbers grow and our methods spread to other competent, dedicated people. All of us are doing this in different ways in different parts of North America.

The problem remains huge; the schools are, for the most part, disinterested in our work despite its track record. One of the options is simply to create a large number of learning centers across both nations. Select a number of intelligent individuals, especially those who would like to be teachers but cannot find an opportunity, and help them establish their own centers. Perhaps if we reach some critical mass in terms of helping large numbers of children and adults, our work will begin to be adopted by public institutions. That will be a part of my efforts in the coming years. These technologies need to be handed down to another generation of practitioners, either inside or outside of mainstream education. We must put in place the means for future generations to teach your children well.

Part Seven

• •

Conclusion

Teach Your Children Well

• •

"A journey of a thousand leagues begins with a single step."
- Lao-tzu

Jamie is a fetching little nine-year-old who is currently a student at my Summer School. He's an adorable-looking child with a personality to match. His smile would melt even the most hardened heart. Last week, a colleague of mine summed it up best when, after meeting and observing Jamie for a few days, he said, "He's the kind of kid you just want to kiss on the forehead."

When he was just four-months-old, Jamie had an allergic reaction to an inoculation. He went into anaphylactic shock, had a seizure and suffered a stroke. A CT scan indicated brain damage, primarily affecting his short-term memory and gross motor skills. His family, of course, was devastated.

Between the ages of 2 and 4, Jamie traveled to a hospital for speech therapy. The teachers at his preschool wanted to label him mentally retarded, but his mother would have no part of it.

In order for him to have every opportunity to achieve and hopefully exceed his potential, she enrolled him in kindergarten in the regular public school system. At age 6, he underwent extensive psychometric testing which, among other discouraging prognoses, predicted that Jamie would never learn how to read.

Every year it was recommended that Jamie be placed in a special class. Every year his mother refused.

What little instruction he received in reading came in the form of the Whole Language approach. Phonics were not in fashion; they were a thing of the past. As a result of continual repetition of the same material, it was hoped that he would eventually begin to recognize words and would start putting them together into sentences. In spite of having a full-time educational assistant, it just didn't happen.

As of January, 1998, nearly four years of schooling had failed to teach Jamie any appropriate academic skills. In February, he began to come to me as a tutorial student for three one-hour weekly sessions in reading. Starting at the entry level of the first Direct Instruction reading program, he learned to sound out individual sounds like "a", "m" and "r". By May, he had completed all 100 lessons and his first "year" of a reading curriculum. At the end of July, he was through the second book of the D.I. Reading Mastery program. He had finished another hundred lessons and was reading 800-word stories about ghosts and genies. He is not yet a fluent reader but he can perform as well as any proficient Grade 2 pupil. Since he is now going into Grade 4, he will continue to be a reading student until he is totally competent. Then we'll tackle spelling and math.

Because of his medical problems, Jamie has less motor control than most nine-year-olds, so his writing is slow and laborious. As a result, each workbook assignment is a major task and can take him up to an hour to complete. He's an avid hockey card collector, and that drives him to get his work done so that he earns his next pack of cards at the end of each lesson.

During his second week at summer school, Jamie arrived one morning with an extra book. It was a present - a World Wrestling Federation jumbo-sized journal. He was almost electric with excitement as he flipped through the pages, showing me his heroes and trying to read the articles about them. I asked him how he had come to get such a fine present and a sly smile crossed his face. He set the wrestling book aside and proudly opened his reading workbook. His grin got bigger and bigger as I thumbed through a dozen pages of homework. After he had left his hour's session with me the previous morning, he had gone home and completed *six* more lessons of the program with his baby-sitter, practice sheets included! I was flabbergasted. Jamie's joy and pride with his accomplishment almost brought tears to my eyes. I immediately declared it "Doubles Day", and presented him with two packs of hockey cards. A few minutes later my visiting friend, Emmet, popped his head into our room and I explained what Jamie had done. "You better give that boy a chocolate bar!" were the first words out of his mouth. "Wow," said Jamie, "two sets of cards AND a chocolate bar. This is my lucky day!"

Luck has very little to do with Jamie's outstanding success story. The use of a sound instructional program combined with an empirically proven measurement system and good behavior management is making Jamie something he was never expected to become - a skillful and competent reader. Who says you cannot *Teach your Children Well?*

Appendix
of
Suggested Readings

Carnine, D., & Silbert, G. (1979). *Direct Instruction Reading*. Columbus, OH: Charles E. Merrill. ISBN 0-675-08277-3.

Colfax, D., & Colfax, M. (1988). *Homeschooling for Excellence: How To Take Charge Of Your Child's Education And Why You Absolutely Must*. New York: Warner Books. ISBN 0-445-38986-2.

Crandall, J., Jacobson, J., & Sloane, H. (eds.), (1997). *What Works in Education*. Cambridge, MA: Cambridge Center for Behavioral Studies. ISBN 1-881317-05-06.

Engelmann, S. (1969). *Preventing Failure in the Primary Grades*. Chicago, Illinois: Science Research Associates.

Engelmann, S. (1992). *War Against The Schools' Academic Child Abuse*. Portland, Oregon: Halcyon House. ISBN 0-89420-287-1.

Finn, Chester E. Jr. (1991). *We Must Take Charge: Our Schools And Our Future*. New York: Free Press, MacMillan, Inc. ISBN 0-02-910275-8.

Hirsch, E.D. (1996). *The Schools We Need and Why We Don't Have Them*. New York: Doubleday. ISBN 0-385-484457-7.

Kozol, Jonathan. (1986). *Illiterate America*. Garden City, New York: Anchor Press, Doubleday. ISBN 0-38519536-2.

Nikiforuk, Andrew. (1993). *School's Out, The Catastrophe in Public Education and What We Can Do About It*. Toronto, Ontario: MacFarlane, Walter and Ross. ISBN 0-921912-48-X.

Nikiforuk Andrew. (1994). *If Learning is so Natural, Why am I going to School? - A Parent's Guide*. Toronto, Ontario: Penguin Books. ISBN 0-14-024264-3.

Silbert, J., Carnine, D., & Stein, M. (1981). *Direct Instruction Mathematics*. Columbus, Ohio: Charles E. Merrill. ISBN 0-675-08047-9.

Taylor, Barbara, O., & Bullard, P. (1995). *The Revolution Revisited: Effective Schools and Systemic Reform*. Bloomington, IN: Phi Delta Kappa Educational Foundation. ISBN 0-87367-483-9.

West, Richard, P., & Hamerlynck, L.A. (eds.). (1992). *Designs for Excellence in Education: The Legacy of B.F.Skinner*. Longmont, Colorado: Sopris West Inc. ISBN 0-944584-52-7.

References

Anderson, A. / *Financial Post*. (Oct. 23, 1994). Toronto, Ontario.

Anderson, R.C., Hiebert, E.F., Scott, J.A., & Wilkinson, I.A.G. (1985). *Becoming A Nation of Readers: The Report of the Commission on Reading.* Washington, DC: The National Institute of Education.

Bateman, B., Chair. *Academic Child Abuse.* Eugene, OR: The Study Group, International Institute for Advocacy for School Children.

Beck, R., & Clement, D. (1976). *Precision Teaching in Review, 1973-1976.* Great Falls, MT: Great Falls Public Schools.

Beck, R., Conrad, D., & Anderson, P. (1995). *Basic Skill Builders Handbook.* Longmont, Colorado: Sopris West. ISBN 1-57035-048-5.

Becker, W.C., Engelmann, S., & Thomas D.R. (1976). *Teaching 1: Classroom Management.* Chicago, IL: Science Research Associates. ISBN 0-574-23035-1.

Becker. W.C., & Carnine, D.W. (1980). Direct Instruction: An effective approach to educational intervention with the disadvantaged and low performers. In Lahey, B.B., & Kazdin, A.K. (eds.). *Advances in Clinical and Child Psychology.* Vol. 3. New York: Plenum.

Becker, W.C., & Carnine, D.W. (1981). Direct Instruction: A behavior theory model for comprehensive educational intervention with the disadvantaged. *Behavior Modification: Contributions to Education.* 145 - 210. Hillsdale, NJ: Lawrence Erlbaum Associates.

Benton, L., & Noyelle T. (1992). *Adult Illiteracy and Economic Performance.* Paris, France: Organization for Educational Research and Innovation, Organization for Economic Co-operation and Development. ISBN 92-64-13597-9.

Bereiter, C., & Kurland, M. (1981). A constructive look at Follow Through results. *Interchange.* 12, 1-22.

Binder, C. (1996). Behavioral Fluency: Evolution of a New Paradigm. *Behavior Analyst.* No.2, (Fall). 163 - 197.

Bock, G., Stebbins, L.B., & Proper, E.C. (1977). *Education as Experimentation: A Planned Variation Model. Vol IV-A, Effects of Follow Through Models.* U.S. Office of Education.

Brookover, W.B., & Lezotte, L.W. (1977). *Changes in school characteristics coincident with changes in student achievement*. East Lansing, MI: Institute for Research on Teaching, Michigan State University.

Bullard, P., & Taylor, B.O. (1993). *Making School Reform Happen*. New York: Allyn & Bacon.

Cairns, J.C. (1988). *Adult Literacy in Canada*. Toronto, Ontario: Council of Ministers of Education.

Carnine, D., & Silbert J. (1979). *Direct Instruction Reading*. Columbus, Ohio: Charles E. Merrill Publishing Co. ISBN 0-675-08277-3.

Carnine, D. (1981). Changes in special education test scores. Personal communication, Toronto, Ontario: York University.

Coalition for Education Reform. (1994). *Could Do Better: What's Wrong With Public Education In Ontario And How To Fix It*. Toronto, Ontario: Coalition For Education Reform.

Coleman, P., & LaRocque, L. (1991). *Struggling to Be Good Enough*. London: Falmer Press.

Coulson, G. (1994). *Power Teaching: How to Find Someone Who Can Teach Your Child When The Education System Fails*. Milton, Ontario: Coulson Press.

Dixon, R.C. (1993). *The Surefire Way to Better Spelling: A Revolutionary New Approach to Turn Poor Spellers into Pros*. New York: St. Martin's Press. ISBN 0-312-09481-7.

Duffy, Francis, M. (1996). *Designing High Performance Schools: A Practical Guide to Organizational Reengineering*. Delray Beach, Florida: St. Lucie Press. ISBN 1-57444-010-1.

Economic Council of Canada. (1992). *A Lot To Learn: Education and Training in Canada*. Ottawa, Ontario.

Engelmann, S. (1969). *Preventing Failure in the Primary Grades*. Chicago, Illinois: Science Research Associates.

Engelmann, S., & Carnine, D. (1982). *Theory of Instruction: Principles and Applications*. New York: Irvington Publishers. ISBN 0-8290-0977-9.

Engelmann, S., Haddox, P., & Bruner, E. (1983). *Teach Your Child to Read in 100 Easy Lessons*. New York: Fireside Press, Simon and Schuster Inc. ISBN 0- 346-12557-X.

Engelmann, S. (1992). *War Against The Schools' Academic Child Abuse*. Portland, Oregon: Halcyon House. ISBN 0-89420-287-1.

Finn, C.E. Jr. (1991). *We Must Take Charge: Our Schools and Our Future*. New York: Free Press, MacMillan Inc. ISBN 0-02-910275-8.

Freedman, J. (1993). *Failing Grades: Canadian Schooling in a Global Economy, Redirecting Canada's Educational Debate*. Red Deer, Alberta: Society for Advancing Educational Research, Full Court Press Inc. ISBN-O-9696939-2-3.

Freedman, J., & Holmes, M. (1993). *Failing Grades - A Videotape*. Red Deer, Alberta: Society for Advancing Educational Research. 0-9696939-0-7.

Freedman, J. (1996). *Charter Schools in Ontario: An Idea Whose Time Has Come*. Unionville, Ontario: Blueline Printing for the Ontario Coalition for Education Reform. ISBN 0-9681151-0-1.

Graf, Stephen, A. (1989). *PracticeSheeter User's Guide*. Youngstown, Ohio: Zero Bros. Software.

Graf, Stephen, A. (1994). *How to Develop, Produce and Use SAFMEDS in Education and Training*. Youngstown, Ohio: Youngstown State University.

Hirsch, E.D. Jr. (1996). *The Schools We Need and Why We Don't Have Them*. New York: Doubleday. ISBN 0-385-484457-7.

House, E.R., Glass, G.V., McLean, L.D., & Walker, D.F. (1978). No Simple Answer: A Critique of the Follow Through evaluation. *Harvard Educational Review*, 48 (2), 128 -159.

Istance, D. (1992). *High Quality Education and Training For All*. Paris, France: Organization for Economic Co-operation and Development. ISBN 92-64-13778-5.

Kirsch, I.S., & Jungeblut, A. (1986). *Literacy: Profiles of America's Young Adults, Final Report*. (Report No. 16 - Pl - 01). Princeton, New Jersey.

Kline, C. *The Globe and Mail*. Dec. 11, 1992. Toronto, Ontario.

Kozol, Jonathan. (1986). *Illiterate America*. Garden City, New York: Anchor Press, Doubleday. ISBN 0-38519536-2.

Ladd, H. (ed.). (1996). *Holding Schools Accountable: Performance Based Reform in Education*. New York: Brookings Institute.

Lindsley, O.R. (1972). *From Skinner to precision teaching: The child knows best*. In Jordan, J.B., & Robbins L.S. (eds.). *Let's try doing something else kind of thing*. (pp. 1 - 11). Arlington Va: Council for Exceptional Children.

Lindsley, O.R. (1982). On the Effects of Charting on Student Progress. Personal Communication.

Lindsley, O.R. (1994 -1995). *Standard Celeration Introduction Kit* (SCIK-2). Lawrence, Kansas: Behavior Research Co.

Maloney, M. (1982). Teaching the Standard Behavior Chart: A Direct Instruction Approximation. *Journal of Precision Teaching*. Vol. 2(4).

Maloney, M., and Humphrey, J.E. (1982). The Quinte Learning Centre: A Successful Venture in Behavioral Education - an Interview with Michael Maloney. *The Behavioral Educator*. 4(1), 1 - 3.

Maloney, M.J., & Summers, H.M. (1986). *Math Tutor* - Addition. New York: Scholastic Inc. ISBN 0-590-97076 -3.

Maloney, M.J., & Summers, H.M. (1986). *Math Tutor* - Subtraction. New York: Scholastic Inc. ISBN 0-590-97076 -3.

Maloney, M.J., & Summers, H.M. (1986). *Math Tutor* - Multiplication. New York: Scholastic Inc. ISBN 0-590-97076 -3.

Maloney, M.J., & Summers, H.M. (1986). *Math Tutor* - Division. New York: Scholastic Inc. ISBN 0-590-97076 -3.

Maloney, M.J., & Summers, H.M. (1986). *Math Tutor* - Fractions. New York: Scholastic Inc. ISBN 0-590-97076 -3.

Maloney, M.J., & Summers, H.M. (1986). *Math Tutor* - Fractions, Decimals and Percents. New York: Scholastic Inc. ISBN 0-590-97076 -3.

Maloney, M.J., & Summers, H.M. (1986). *Math Tutor* - Ratios and Equations. New York: Scholastic Inc. ISBN 0-590-97076 -3.

Maloney, M.J., & Summers, H.M. (1984). *Mighty Math*. Toronto, Ontario: Scholastic Inc. ISBN 0-590-97076 -3.

Maloney, M., Desjardins, A., & Broad, P. (1990). Teach Your Children Well. *Journal of Precision Teaching*. 7(2), 36 - 58.

McCuen, G. E. (1988). *Illiteracy in America*. Hudson, Wisconsin: GEM Publications Inc.

Nadler, Richard. (1998). Failing Grade. *National Review*. Vol. L, No. 8, p. 38.

Nikiforuk, Andrew. (1993). *School's Out: The Catastrophe in Public Education and What We Can Do About It*. Toronto, Ontario: MacFarlane, Walter and Ross. ISBN 0-921912-48-X.

O'Neill, P.G. (1988). Teaching Effectiveness: A Review of the Research. *Canadian Journal of Education*. 13.1, 162-185.

Osborne, Steve. (1988). *Reading Mastery Series Guide*. Chicago, Illinois: Science Research Associates, Inc. ISBN 0-574-10222-1.

Pennypacker, H.S., & Hench, L.L. (1997). Making behavioral technology transferable. *The Behavior Analyst*, Vol. 20, No. 2, 97 - 108. ISSN 0738-6729.

Q.E.D. (1997-98). *The Education Market Guide & Mailing List Catalog*. p.10. Denver, Colorado: Quality Education Data.

Rand Corporation. (1982). Declining S.A.T. Scores in Education and Other Professions. *T.H.E. Technical Horizons in Education Journal*. Vol.10, No. 4.

Raspberry, William. (1998). What Works: Education establishment slow to learn from successes, failures. *Washington Post*. Washington, DC.

Rippa, S. A. (1992). *Education in a Free Society*. White Plains, New York: Longman's.

Stevenson, H. (1992). *In Failing Grades*. (1993). A Videotape. Red Deer, Alberta: Society for Advancing Educational Research.

Sulzer-Azaroff, B. (1998). *Who killed my daddy? A behavioral safety fable*. Cambridge, MA: Cambridge Center for Behavioral Studies.

Taylor, B.O., & Bullard, P. (1993). *Making School Reform Happen*. Bloomington, Indiana: Phi Delta Kappa Educational Foundation.

Taylor, B.O., & Bullard, P. (1995). *The Revolution Revisited: Effective Schools and Systemic Reform*. Bloomington, Indiana: Phi Delta Kappa Educational Foundation. ISBN 0-87367-483-9.

Toch, T. (1991). *In the Name of Excellence: The Struggle to Reform the Nation's Schools, Why It's Failing and What Should Be Done*. New York: Oxford University Press.

Watkins, C.L. (1997). *Project Follow Through: A Case Study of Contingencies Influencing Instructional Practices of the Educational Establishment*. Cambridge, MA: Cambridge Center for Behavioral Studies. ISBN 1-881317-04-8.

West, R.P., & Hamerlynck, L.A. (eds.). (1992). *Designs for Excellence in Education: The Legacy of B.F. Skinner*. Longmont, Colorado: Sopris West Inc. ISBN 0-944584-52-7.

Index

IF YOU BUILD IT, THEY WILL COME

LEARNING SUCCESS

Within Every Child's Reach

EDUCATIONAL SERVICES

Would you like to teach children and adults to read, write, spell and do math?

Do you have a son or daughter who would love to be a teacher, but is unable to enroll in a Teachers' College?

Open a learning center. We can help. We have 20 years experience in site selection, staff training, advertising, marketing, financing and managing.

Call, fax or e-mail Michael Maloney today to find out more about securing a QLC Educational Services Learning Center license.

IS YOUR GROUP INTERESTED IN EDUCATIONAL ISSUES LIKE:

- literacy
- reading
- math
- spelling
- effective teaching methods
- risk of school failure
- special education
- school accountability
- adult education
- educational software

Do you need a speaker for meetings, conferences, symposiums, workshops or keynotes?

Contact Michael Maloney at:

QLC Educational Services
217 Pinnacle Street, P.O. Box 908
Belleville, Ontario, Canada
K8N 5B6

Phone: (613) 967-9959
Fax: (613) 967-3752
Website: http://www.qlced.com
e-mail: info@qlced.com

Arithmetic, typing, keypad skills;
other programs
soon to be announced!

**Check out our
"Learn and Earn" Program at:**

http://www.CyberSlate.ca